VANILLA
SLIM

An Improbable Pimp in the
Empire of Lust

BOB ARMSTRONG

CARROLL & GRAF PUBLISHERS
NEW YORK

VANILLA SLIM
An Improbable Pimp in the Empire of Lust

Carroll & Graf Publishers
An Imprint of Avalon Publishing Group Inc.
245 West 17th Street
11th Floor
New York, NY 10011

AVALON
publishing group incorporated

Copyright © 2006 by Bob Armstrong

First Carroll & Graf edition 2006

Library of Congress Cataloging-in-Publication Data is available.

ISBN-13: 978-0-78671-701-9
ISBN-10: 0-7867-1701-7

9 8 7 6 5 4 3 2 1

Interior Design by Maria E. Torres
Printed in the United States of America
Distributed by Publishers Group West

For Mahrie

An index card with a quotation from George Orwell stuck atop my computer served as Big Brother while I wrote this book:

"Autobiography is only to be trusted when it reveals something disgraceful. A man who gives a good account of himself is probably lying, since any life when viewed from the inside is simply a series of defeats."

While bad behavior should not be trumpeted as more authentic than good, I hope my spooled-out adventures into the darkest corner of the sex industry will add up to something more than my fingerprints on a police blotter.

PROLOGUE

I ended up in the slammer. Sitting in a holding cell at the county jail in a pool of my own sweat and fear, one thought raced through my brain: Prison. Two, three, five years? Then again, maybe I'd walk with probation and a fine, this being libertine San Francisco where my crime—pimping—is sometimes viewed as an accommodating vice.

The big trouble began with a knock on my office door while I was talking to a shy young man who spends most of his life playing chess on the Internet. He wanted more than a quick sex fix with one of my eye-busting escorts. While assuring him that Havana, a blossomy cutie with a cupcake bottom, would give him plenty of time, I opened the door to be greeted by a shiny gold police badge.

Two plain-clothed vice cops pushed inside, one a handsome young man with serial seducer eyes and a classic cop jaw, the other a gruff-looking older dude who looked as if he tracked down wild animals for breakfast. The hungry heavyweight cuffed me, said I was under arrest for running girls. In an emotionless drone, the younger fuzz read me my rights. He then poked about the office while the sledgehammer, who was very polite, interrogated me.

I admitted I ran an escort service but lied about money for sex. He knew it was a lie, let it pass, acted as if he was just curious, wanted the inside scoop on how an escort service works, laughed when I told him I was "really just a facilitator of liaisons for the socially challenged."

Our conversation was interrupted by a chirping noise. I winced. The cop grabbed my cell phone off the desk, stuck it to his ear. "Hello . . . Bob? . . . Sorry, he can't come to the phone, he's tied up right now," he said, winking and flashing me a big grin.

Since the person on the phone had asked for me by name, I figured it was one of the girls, possibly Havana. Sledgehammer kept the conversation going, said he just started working for me. "I guess I haven't met you yet, but I've heard good things about you from Bob."

Before the smooth flatfoot could reel her in, I yelled at the top of my lungs: *"Cops!"*

The young cop, in the midst of rummaging through manila folders in a cardboard box labeled "sex stories," swung around and glowered at me. "Don't even think about doing something like that again," he warned.

Sledgehammer put my cell phone in his jacket pocket, sighed, gave me a we-were-getting-along-so-well look. "Now, that's not the way to behave, is it?"

We both shook our heads in unison. "How much money you making?" he asked.

"Two, sometimes three grand a month," I replied.

He seemed skeptical, his partner even more so, wondering aloud if twenty grand a month might be closer to the mark. (Later, when I told a friend how much money I made, she too was flabbergasted: "You couldn't even turn big bucks in the world's oldest profession? That's the *real* crime!")

In the backseat of a patrol car taking me to jail, I wished for a head-on collision with a truck for a total wipeout. I wanted to die, and if a couple of cops went with me, so much the better.

I'll say this for jail. It's the right vibe to ponder your fuck-ups. The place stank like a cat litter box. A stale, sharp-smelling wino was snoring contentedly on his cot, his crusty feet covered with deep skin lesions, a wart on his leg as black as vermin. From the running sores on this downtown untouchable's body to the scummy sealed windows above, the cellblock was filled with the odor of anger, sorrow, pain, disease, and despair.

Almost everybody can sympathize with the down and out behind bars. Among the criminal class, you can even make the case a serial killer or a child molester is the victim of abuse. You can shift the blame on society, or culture, or class, or The Man. Not so with foul smells. There is something fundamentally nauseating about human stinkpots. You can't get past the smell, can't blame it on an abstraction.

I kept moving about, but no matter where I turned, rank stink invaded my nostrils. The icing on this contaminated cake was a scene that we have all witnessed, an overflowing toilet, its collective excreta swirling in a dark, turbid sea that swept away all hope of privacy, civility, and cleanliness. Just condemnation, I suppose, and I did feel like a shit, a turd with eyes gazing at the snoring beggar's pockmarked face, his matted gray hair falling down past his eyes, his thin, bluish emphysema-tinged lips dreaming of an oxygen tank.

So I closed my eyes and tried to overcome the stench by thinking about sweet smells, fresh winds blowing across the beach on the Oregon coast, the fragrant scent of fresh cooked steelhead trout over a campfire. I remembered my childhood days walking up a path lined with red and yellow maple leaves, running through fiddlehead ferns, tossing pinecones at the jays and warblers scattering through the trees. Two red-tailed hawks flew in tandem across the wide sky. A lone eagle circled over my grandmother's place, a dilapidated gray clapboard house bleached by the salty winds, half concealed by thick, twisting honeysuckle vines. Inside the house, a huge stone fireplace in the living room was stoked with logs, the kitchen smelled of homemade bread rising in deep metal bowls, and high drafty steps led to a musty attic filled with steamer trunks and other treasures.

I'd rummage around the attic, watch the cobweb architects at work, go downstairs and gobble up a slice of homemade bread slathered with peanut butter. Apple pie for dessert. Sometimes dessert outside: My fingers carefully picked through thorns to extract blackberries swollen with juice, or plucked handfuls of huckleberries hidden in the bushes. The scent of ripe berries merged with the smell of the forest filled with oak, pine, cedar, spruce, hemlock, and towering Douglas fir. About a half-mile into the ancient woods, the forest grew darker as I entered the home of spotted owls and woodpeckers nesting in feathery branches; shrews and bushy-tailed wood rats scampering under weathered stumps of fallen trees smothered in moss. Soft mounds of fungi grew fat in well-rotted logs. I liked the smells from all that rich rot.

When the smoldering scent from autumn leaves burning in the backyard died away and the winter winds picked up, I sucked in the cold air, watched the mass of dark clouds surging through the sky. Massive trees crashed in a storm, snags of logs cut across canyons and ravines. The army of woody debris rushed downriver under the high winds, past the sandbar, out into the ocean where the tumbling weight of logs rolled in silvery waters. Soon the play of the night tide hurled the logs back on the empty beach below the lighthouse, a deserted castle of the sea that once guided tall three-masted ships safely through the treacherous waves along the rocky coastline.

I loved walking along the beach during a great winter storm, smelling the crisp air, letting the rain soak me through. Then again, the rain can blind you, sting your skin, and, as they said in Oregon during the outhouse days, when it rains, all your shit goes to your feet. As I opened my eyes, a new smell hung in the air over the jailhouse steel toilet, the pungent odor of powerful disinfectant, a clean latrine hosed down, under control, the malodorous pile of shit a passing reminder of more shit to come.

Seemed like most of the guys in this cellblock were temps

passing through on drunk driving charges, although I did hear a guard mention something about "frequent fliers" with whom he'd dealt on previous occasions. The boozy drivers babbled away in street legalese intelligible only to those intimately familiar with DUI law—all sorts of arguments swirled around about what it took to get a license suspended, the "value" of tickets, the intoxication level, previous stupidities behind the wheel, "points" for this and that.

One character, Valentine Jones, would have been grateful for a DUI. He'd been charged with assault and battery in a gang dispute. He assured me it was self-defense, and perhaps it was, by the looks of him. His misshapen nose was joined to his face at a straight angle, as if it had been broken in a fight, and a cut on one corner of his mouth had left a trace of a scar. Still, Valentine's weapon of choice during the gang fight would stack the deck in favor of any prosecutor. He'd busted three fingers on his opponent's hand with a "Smiley," a padlock on the end of a swinging chain, so named for the imprint it sometimes left on its victim. Other than that, Valentine said little about his case. He did have a keen interest in mine, but thought I was lying.

"Ya bullshittin' me, ya ain't no pimp. Ya look like a lawyer."

"Nope, but tell that to the jury in my defense."

"So if it be real, how ya git in the game?"

"Ran an advertisement under Escorts in the newspaper," I said, then filled him in at length on my operation. I laid it out in a sort of "how to" fashion for his benefit, and he then seemed convinced I be real.

Valentine was stretched out on the top bunk. He pulled himself up and threw his legs over the side. "Damn, a white muthafucka pimp. Ya know, that's cool, fixin' things up at fancy hotels with yo bitches. But ya still messin' with da man. You a very smart dude, I can tell. Betcha got a lotta college, right?"

"Yes, I went to college," I replied guardedly, then quickly added for a prop, "but most of my education was in 'Nam."

"Same with my daddy, he got a court-martial degree over there," he said, dangling his feet over the edge of the bunk bed.

I laughed, made no attempt to top that comeback. Valentine jumped down, stood tall, cocked his head to one side, paused briefly, then dug in. "Problem is, I don't think you got street smarts. That's why you got busted, right?"

I nodded. Valentine became excited, stepped forward, almost in my face. His hair, plastered with a pound of gel and flecked with dandruff, gave off a pungent smell, like talcum powder mixed with rancid butter.

"Gotta know that same shit is gonna happen again, unless you got some backup," he said firmly. "That's my business. We could throw in together, me knowin' if the five-ohs are on the set and how to keep away from da man so's we can score the pussy money without gettin' jammed. I make sure we get what we want when we want it, like always ta-nite, never ta-maura. All right, tell me, that what y'after?"

Valentine stepped back, put his hands on his hips, thrust his chest out. When I saw that young black man standing with total confidence in front of an iron gate, I thought, now here's a smooth operator who is tough, clever, charming, and ambitious. Here stands a man who can cut deals and kiss ass, a man who's fast on his feet and can grab at a possibility on a moment's notice. In short, the "be all that you can be" American dream, even if all this is light-years away from the facts in his case. But I wanted to hear more, and he knew exactly how to bait the hook. *"All right. Tell me, that what y'after?"*

"I'm open to the possibility," I said. "Tell me more about yourself."

Valentine gave me a stern look. "I want you to know I myself ain't no punkass Oaktown nigger runnin' his mouth and messin' with wannabe fools who don't know nothin' and can't even remember the last time they was without a fix. I just say to that sorry ass, git da fuck outta here, man. I got no time for ya. But I ain't perfect neither, and I know I'm supposed to better myself. So's maybe I should go to Merritt College. But—"

"Merritt sounds very good," I interrupted.

Valentine threw up his hands. "Oh man, d'as it, Merritt's the *word* gets shoved up our black asses from Day One. They say, Huey Newton went to Merritt. Well, fuck Huey! Besides, what Merritt do for him? Look where he end up. *Right here,"* he screamed, jabbing his forefinger straight down.

"Merritt, Merritt, Merritt—everybody that's anybody say we got to go to Merritt, and now it's *comin' from a fuckin' pimp.* I'd last about a week at Merritt. Thing is, I'm gonna have to get the bucks and the fucks another way. But lemme tell ya, I ain't no bragman wearing a big diamond ring on my pinkie and ten gold chains around my neck, playing like I'm the coolest Black Pan-thuh pimp ever to be seen on this planet. No, I lay low under the radar."

"No gold chain around your neck, that's cool, but what about that Smiley?"

"Well, I ain't ta be fucked with, but if you're ready to ride, I can whup ass without it."

I'm sure a ride with Valentine would have been quite an adventure. He certainly knew how to load on his strong points in the job interview. I'd like to think that the words flying out of his mouth were not those of a common thug. But whatever was storming through his heart, his fondness for a Smiley would not go down well with the flaming little buds in my escort garden. Or, for that matter, anybody's garden, except in neighborhoods where young men bash each other's lights out as a matter of course.

Shortly after our conversation, the keys rattled against the gate, a guard entered, called out Valentine's name, and escorted him to another cell, perhaps special quarters reserved for Smiley assailants. As he left, Valentine waved my way. "Stay strong," he called.

I did stay strong, for about three minutes, then pulled the blanket up over my head so the other jailbirds could not see my tears. The keys rattled again, followed by a great commotion, more inmate names being called. An exit parade followed, the drunk drivers giggling, apparently figuring they were free, others bitching and moaning, not sure of their next destination. A sullen Native

American, sitting at the end of a long metal table bolted to the floor, carefully watched the countdown. Ten Little Indians crossed my mind, then his name was called, the last to go (Then There Was One). The cage slammed shut, and I remained alone. Even in jail, the victim of affirmative action.

The cell was large, eight bunk beds running down each side, two long tables, the spicy steel toilet, and a thick yellow line down the center of the concrete floor. I figured it would start filling up again soon, got nervous after a few hours ticked away and I was still alone. Some special plan for the white pimp cooking? Was I doomed to forever walk the night in circles, nothing more remaining of me than a pile of blood and meat?

I'm a pacer. At least I was in a good cell for that, I figured. In a figure eight around the tables. Back and forth. High stepping between the bunks. Ooh, that felt good! Marching gyrene style up and down the yellow line, like in boot camp. About-face, a few snappy salutes, fifty pushups, well, seven anyway.

In general, I prefer solitude, but as the hours drifted into the dark, I kept hoping a frequent flier would show and fill me in on his latest crime. Instead, I was left alone with what I feared most: me. As in the real me, but it was time to take the bull by the horns. I must confront the Big Pop. You hear the Big Pop when you pull your head out of your ass. I was forced to conclude that the word I hate most had some merit: change.

Pacing around, I started to sweat. I never sweat, yet I was soaking in it. I stopped pacing at the end of the yellow line, turned around, got down on my hands and knees with my chin a few inches from the floor. I crawled forward as fast as I could, the yellow line leaping ahead of me like a burning fuse: *C'mon, Big Pop, c'mon!*

When I got to the end of the yellow line, I closed my eyes and craned my neck upwards. I did not hear the Big Pop or the sound of one hand clapping. I did not feel the pull of Saturn's rings or see a vision of Jesus. I opened my eyes and saw—a cement wall. I also saw a long brown rusty stain below a capped-off water pipe. I tried and failed to divine its significance.

I returned to the bunk bed, leaned against the side of the top cot, and fell back on the boring anal-retentive method of "thinking it through."

Why did I join the ranks of the pimps?

I used to be active in political circles on the left. Most of my friends were political animals, although I hadn't seen many of them since I turned in my good citizenship card. I was still fascinated by the spectacle of the American Empire growing ever stronger, but the lightness of my mind no longer permitted me to bitch about it. Besides, the empire was a good deal for me, since my lifestyle was not tenable in a civilized society. I was a happy parasite in the belly of the beast.

I still admired people who had principles, but I found myself more in tune with con artists, fakes, frauds, sleazebags. This seems quite natural when your life is a failure. After so many failures with women and in the workplace, you begin to enjoy being on the bottom layer of the social order. Like the junkie finding the last vein in his neck, or the alcoholic opening his throat so the bottle can pour straight down, unencumbered by swallowing. If it is true that we are the sum of all the moments in our lives, all I can say is, long live subtraction.

A classic underachiever, when I hit my fifties, and realized there would be fewer new mornings ahead, I didn't much care about anything. With my life escalating south, pimping seemed like a terrific way to weird up and fly high. At last I found something I was good at. And pimping was addictive.

But I must stop.

ONE

ordelia panics: "I forgot protection," she groans with a clipped British accent.

"Some in the glove compartment," I say on the way to the St. Francis Hotel.

"How proper," Cordelia replies, reaching in and retrieving two Durex Extra Sensitive condoms. She's nervous, looks at me with uncertain eyes. "I hope I can go through with this," she mumbles, while sparking an American Spirit cigarette.

"You'll do fine," I assure her.

A long moment drags by before she says, "It should be easy enough, tossing it off with a stranger. Might even be fun."

Cordelia's ideal for my operation, the Zen Escort Service. She's new to the game and won't be in it for long, visiting San Francisco from London on an extended vacation, perhaps beyond the time limit stamped on her passport. Silky jet-black hair down to her shoulders, clear complexion, potent big brown eyes, a twenty-two-inch waist, insecure for no apparent reason, and flat broke.

I pull slowly around the corner in front of the St. Francis. Cordelia grinds her cigarette out in the ashtray. A point for etiquette: most of the Zen dolls flip them out the window. She reaches up, flips down the visor, and checks her reflection in the mirror. "Do I look okay?"

She does look a bit pale, fear having drawn the color from her cheeks. I lay down a line: "Honey, your face should be on the cover of *Vogue*. You're my number one girl."

She lightly slaps my face. "Bob, you are so not smooth," she intones, then bounces out of the car in a perfumed breeze, moves into the night and disappears between the glass planes of the revolving door. Inside, she will nod politely to the night concierge and head to a rendezvous of a sort that has animated the history of this city since the Gold Rush.

The trick is out here on business from Baltimore. He's a financial consultant, whatever that means. Mr. Baltimore must have some bucks, because Zen charges $500 an hour, almost double the fee of most escort services in the city. I don't get as much business, but a high end operation draws better clients, and I'm able to attract the best-looking girls into Zen.

I drive up the hill to a quiet, dark street in front of Grace Cathedral, and wait for the hour to roll by. Nobody around. Bill Evans on KCSM's *Jazz After Hours*. I gingerly lay out a line of speed on the back cover of Mary McCarthy's *The Company She Keeps*, published in 1942, the year I was born.

I wonder if Mr. Baltimore looks like "something out of a seed catalogue"—that's McCarthy's description of a middle-aged traveling salesman a young girl meets on a train to Portland, the city I left long ago. Despite his appearance, the young girl does the deed with him in a Pullman compartment as the train hurtles past the Great Salt Lake, an area of "sterility, polygamy, and waste."

I snort the line of speed to rally my energies. Bill Evans's piano paints true colors in the night sky over the cathedral. But no orange colors. I hate orange.

I've never been a heavy drug user, but after complaining about lack of sleep, one of the Zen dolls offered me a pick-me-upper. Nice reverse play there, the ho hooking the pimp.

Always behind the curve on drugs, after I returned from Vietnam, I regretted never having tasted a sample from Uncle Ho's Victory Garden (although in a war zone, it's always best to remain on full alert). I tried a variety of drugs after washing off the war dirt, but except for pot, the pharmacopoeial goodies never did much for me.

And such delicious options: Xanax, Zoloft, THC, DMA, STP, LSD, 'ludes, glue, smack, snow, blow, green uppers, blue downers, and red lead.

Never could bust out of reality like those in the pantheon of the Radiant Glow: William Burroughs on yage watching larval beings pass before his eyes; Terence McKenna transformed by a tab of Orange Sunshine into an ultra-high-frequency orgasmic goblin; Aleister Crowley soaked in cognac, love, and coke; Iceberg Slim daggering the needle in his pimp vein; Bayard Taylor puffing hashish, drifting helplessly through a gorgeous web of a thousand rainbows;

Aldous Huxley on mescaline contemplating the sumptuous red sur-
faces of books glowing in a corner of his room; Ernst Jünger gazing
at red-violet roses and white chrysanthemums flaring up and
sending out lightning flashes along a string of glass beads; Thomas
DeQuincey in the Depths below Depths; Alan Watts surging
through the Center of Centers; Timothy Leary and Richard Alpert
tuning into messages from high-flying Radar Beings in the Beyond;
and Hunter S. Thompson french-frying his brain while tromping
on the pedal of his Great Red Shark heading to somewhere around
Barstow.

Wish I'd been there.

Then again, my current condition unequivocally suggests I best
leave these journeys to others. Crystal methamphetamine has served
its purpose all too well. Sometimes, I can write like the wind on
speed, but all too often I'm just wasted on the stuff, night and day
blending into oblivion.

The hour's almost over. I snag another line, head down the hill, and
scope out a tart in the Tenderloin leaning on one leg up against a
wall. I pull over and park, remembering Cordelia had mentioned she
likes Arizona Iced Tea. The Zen crew has respective favorite soda
pops, and I make sure the correct selection awaits them after turning
a trick. I grab a bottle at the Cadillac Market on the corner of Hyde
and Eddy.

The Pakistani behind the cash register—or maybe he's from

India, I can never nail the correct language around that hostile border—starts to bag it. I shake my head with ecological piety, scoop up the bottle, and walk out, where I'm greeted by the eager-eyed wall girl. Time has torn up her face. Eyes lost in puffy fat pur-plish rings, slack body, sallow complexion, her mouth a deep ditch. There's so little life left in her, I swear stretch marks are running up her high heels.

In her polluted river, the splendor and the sadness of the Tender-loin rushes on. Once beautiful with dark eyes big enough to wade in, now a naked cry in the dark. "Get your crazy ass outta my face," she screams at a panhandler who actually pops up in my face, not hers.

Swaying like a sailor on a rope ladder, he points a cruddy finger toward her and barks, "I was talkin' to him, not you, bitch."

Her head jerks forward on her thin neck. "Well, *I'm* talking to him, and we don't want to be disturbed." She places her hands on her hips, throws her shoulders back, her slack body now almost attractive. The panhandler moves on, then turns around and yells, "She's got AIDS."

She windmills an index finger toward him. "You got the AIDS. Every dick in the Castro's been cummin' up your ass." She turns back to me with a satisfied smile. "So, whatcha up to?"

I appreciate her intervention, but that's all. "On my way to the airport. Going to Pakistan on the red-eye."

She shoots me an annoyed glance. "Why you lying to me?"

"I never lie. I'm with the CIA. Got a dangerous operation going down in Karachi."

"Wanna date before your danger? I'm clean, no HIV or nothin'."

I pull a five out of my pocket and slip it in her hand. "Against CIA regs, but I can donate to your nonprofit therapy organization."

"Thanks," she says, embracing me. Her eyelids half-closed, her big broad-lipped mouth moves close to mine, and she adds a nice melodramatic touch with a husky tone of voice: "Be careful in Pak-stan."

Off she goes into the shifting shadows. Might this daughter of joy have AIDS? Probably not, but in the Tenderloin the bottom layer seems surrounded by an aura of syph, clap, gutterlust, and the plus. Really, it's the past that has infected the TL, the anonymous dust kicked up by generations of outcasts plunging forward into the atmosphere of this neighborhood that never forgives.

Here in the TL, the cop cars cruise slowly along Ellis or Jones or Turk, knowing they can make a bust on any corner. Yet, as soon as a black-and-white comes into view, the street is almost empty. The gangsters and vagrants seem to slide into the cracks in the pavement. The Mom & Pop grocery stores sell forty-ouncers, and welfare cases hock food stamps five for two. Tourists from Dresden and Tokyo who neglected to follow the proper Fisherman's Wharf and cable car map gawk at six-foot trannies with padding in their asses sashaying up Larkin.

There's enough outstanding bench warrants among the halfway house parolees, pedophiles in SROs (single residence occupancy), and methadone outpatients to fill 850 Bryant ten times over. Simply to live here comes off as a punishable offense. Repeated attempts at improving the neighborhood have failed over three decades, but glorious blueprints for glittering gentrification spring up about every thirty days. Fat chance. The sun will shine at midnight before the TL is gentrified.

Then again, I sometimes sense the midnight sun—always a possibility in this city of dreams—is now shining over the Tenderloin. A continual stream of flowers falls from the sky, brightening the cruddy streets, red and yellow petals unfolding and whirling over the clanging bells atop Glide Memorial Church, fine flowers with singsong names like Trung My Hung, Than Thi Lan, Le Quang Mia, and Nguyen Thi Cuc.

Say what you will about America's bloodbucket strategy in Vietnam, but the aftermath brought in boatloads of hard-working future citizens. For many Vietnamese who made it over the treacherous seas, the TL became their new home. Ratty boarded-up storefronts sprang to life with a fresh coat of paint, new furnishings, and the proud sweat of determined refugees. Hazily lit fish tanks glow in the darkened interior of the Ocean Flower Aquarium, the pungent air of spices fills the doorway of the Meng Tak Herbs & Ginseng shop, fresh vegetables await customers at Heip Thanh Foods; dozens of cafés and restaurants serve steamy pho soup, crisp Imperial rolls, and strong filtered coffee floating on a sea of sweet condensed milk. A statue of Buddha sits serenely on emerald-colored tapestry in a jewelry store, the scent of joss sticks smoldering on a window ledge, a South Vietnamese flag flutters off a fire escape in the morning breeze.

Tonight, the vacant eyes of the streetwalker look back at me one more time, a little wave of the hand, then she crosses the street and waves again to a passing car. It pulls over. She runs to the passenger side, gets in. As the car rolls past me, she sticks her arm out the window and gives me a thumbs-up. Girl's on a roll, her midnight sun ablaze.

Parked in front of the St. Francis, I wait for Cordelia, notice the engine on my oil-leaking '85 Dodge is idling precariously. I hang on to the dented gold-colored heap, knowing it's doomed. Years ago, when I lived in Albuquerque, the Dodge was abandoned in my driveway by a junkie friend whose parents flew him back to Dallas for a fourth or fifth round of rehab. Never heard from him again, so I suspect the intervention flopped. I don't much care what I drive, yet quickly get attached to a set of wheels. I remain loyal until the mechanic says it's time for a valve job. Then: sayonara.

A Luxor Cab pulls to the curb in front of my gold pile. Miss Advertise Myself as a Prostitute steps out in four-inch white high heels and a way-too-tight pink skirt over her humongous ass. She's got enough bleach in her dubious blonde hair to clean all the junkies' rigs in town. Coming out of the hotel, Cordelia passes by the pink siren as she's wobbling in. "Awfully bold, don't you think?" she asks as she gets into the car.

Her face is relaxed, and color has returned to her cheeks. I smell the freshness of her silky long hair as I hand her the Arizona Iced Tea. "Oooh, how considerate," she coos, twisting off the cap.

"For the fairest of them all," I roar in a Brit accent.

She rolls her eyes, hands me my cut ($150) and shows me a finger-sized container of shampoo. "I asked if I could have it. He laughed, said sure, then ran his hand over his bald head. I told him it's what's inside that head that matters, and he liked that."

"Nice move."

"Well, I do believe that. I mean, it wasn't intended as manipulation, but, uh, I realize that escorting does involve manipulating people. I'm not sure I can think of any job that doesn't."

"For sure. Compared to other businesses, Zen isn't that manipulative. It's truth in packaging."

"Packaging? You're terrible," she laughs, lights a cig, her nose even more perky under the flare. "I had the feeling when I saw the word Zen in the ads that it would be . . . I don't know, really, somehow different. And you are different. Why did you pick the name?"

"You answered your own question. Different, a bit mysterious. It's a word with pull—a word people use all the time, with only a vague idea of what it means. Like, 'he's zenned out,' almost like he's spaced out on some sort of wavelength preventing him from making a trip to the grocery store for a bag of Doritos. At the same time, almost everybody is clued in to Zen as something Kung Fu'd and orange-robed. Really, it's not spaced out. Zen is a way of seeking enlightenment through introspection. Didn't you toss off some enlightenment while on the clock?"

"Oh yes, a blow job is always enlightening," Cordelia snaps back, her singsong words running out behind the smoke. "Oh, you have

M People!" she squeals, rummaging through my cassettes. "I went to one of their concerts in London." She slaps in the tape and sings along to "Search for the Hero." Over the maxed-out volume she asks if I can drop her at the Ten 15 Club.

I buzz into SOMA, alternative culture turf occupied by slick hip-hop blades, chi-chi demimondes, and Cuban-heeled renegades. They jostle in long lines, funneling into the nightclubs where dee-jays cut and paste their decks with electro funk, progressive trance, industrial death rock, reggae, old school rap, hip-hop, hip-slop, and deep tech house. All crap to my ears. This chunk of the city, once filled with army surplus stores, auto repair shops, hardware stores, longshoremen's bars and union halls, has been overwhelmed by the new groove.

Trouble is, grooves never cease to groove. The young art rock crowd is now under siege from a slightly older crowd of workaholics with platinum cards, moving into new half-million-dollar lofts. They hate the club noise in the wee hours. Face-off time. Go-between committees of progressive guitar players, property owners, city planners, and cops negotiate and renegotiate decibel ordinances. The fight goes on.

I pull up in front of Ten 15. Cordelia gives me a peck on the cheek and hops out. Zen returns to silence, as she fades into dance-land under the colored lights.

This British babe is one of the brighter bulbs in the escort biz. By and large, women who turn tricks barely made it through high school, more likely dropouts. This is most damaging when a cute

Lolita opts for permanent truancy, and ends up under the thumb of a street pimp. Good looks and bad grades can be a potent combination. In the worst case scenario, this leads to ten-minute quickies at $30 a pop on Capp Street. Frequently, these minors have been sexually abused by Daddy, Stepdaddy, or sly old Uncle Ted with a four-stool bar and an L-shaped Naugahyde couch in his rumpus room. The young girls gradually become accustomed to chewing Altoids after a blow job and turning their money over to a rotten-toothed pimp with a long rap sheet. In return, they have a "safe" place to live and plenty of smack to keep them pliant.

Most of the street girls are black. You don't need stats to prove that. Confirmation is quite visible on certain streets in every major city. Even when they turn eighteen, "Spade Ballers," a put-down used by black girls in the same profession, have a tough time getting work at escort services. Zen has one sleek stone fox who rarely gets her ticket punched. In part, I suspect, a lot of white guys fear that inviting a black girl over to their condo will quickly be followed by rip city from an iron-fisted 200-pound brother smashing down the door.

Race aside, the pain and sadness endured by street kittens is spread about with equal opportunity. Shannon, a stubborn imprudent blonde, found this out when she ran away from home at fourteen. The perfect target for the pimp's poison arrow.

TWO

The cell phone's on my ear as the golden pile rumbles into the Mission. "Meetcha outside . . . *the fuckin' money didn't just crawl out by itself,*" I hear Shannon scream. She's talking to me while in the midst of a fight with her mother, who had slipped her fingers in Shannon's purse, in need of cash for crack. Mother, thirty-four, and daughter, twenty, are both prostitutes. I've met her mom, who looks pretty good, despite a couple of decades of heroin and cocaine in her veins.

Shannon insisted I not put her mother on the Zen roll. I had no intention of doing so. I'm sure a mother/daughter tag team would appeal to some meatballs, but even a pimp has to draw the line somewhere.

I wouldn't say Shannon was born to hook, but her first steps seemed destined to land on a corner in Hell. The street is the last stop for older burnt-out working girls the cops generally ignore, and the tragic starting point for girls around thirteen or fourteen whom the cops target. Almost all the teeny-boppers eventually get popped. Despite the howlings and tremblings from the progressive nonprofit humanitarian complex, a formidable political force in San Francisco, plenty of public dough streams through numerous nonjudgmental services to assist the girls whose judgmental capacity is zero. A few turn their lives around, but most, like Shannon, continue to track with their sisters of wrath.

In the prostitution industry, like much else in American life, there's an escalator going up and another one going down. Judge this old pimp harshly if so inclined, but Shannon is close to the top of the escalator. (Zen is a step or two below the best setup, an eighty-two-year-old sugar daddy on a pacemaker who owns a string of oil wells outside Fort Worth.)

One night at my place, Shannon took a big bite out of a Baby Ruth and launched into a tale about her mother's pimp in Philadelphia, a long-haired dude with a short list of girls, all living with him. Shannon was seven when she and her mom moved into his stable. She fondly remembers all the girls bouncing through the house, playing with her, combing her golden locks and saying "my, my, such a *beautiful* child."

The little girl liked all that attention, more than she had had in a previous complex family arrangement with a grandmother, several uncles and aunts, and four or five cousins all fighting for food at the dinner table. "That's why I eat so fast. I know I shouldn't, but I can't help it. Lotta times there wasn't enough food, so we had to grab what we could and eat it as fast as possible."

Even more, she liked the attention from the pimp, who showered her with Teddy bears, Barbie dolls, and Baby Ruths. "He was so cool. Giving me presents all the time. One time, he got me this stuffed baby seal, taller than me, all white and so-o-o fluffy. Most all the pimps are black, but this guy was whiter than you, the whitest skin I ever saw. He'd lean his head against the seal, and I swear it was whiter than the seal's. Then he'd eat a candy bar and rub it against the seal's face. That's how I got hooked on these," she'd said, waving the Baby Ruth in my face. "I don't think I ever saw him without a Baby Ruth in his hand. He was a smart guy, knew how to keep things steady. He was pretty nice to my mom and the other girls. He'd yell at 'em, but never hit 'em."

Shannon witnessed the girls coming and going, heard them on the phone buttering up the johns. She felt the hand of her mother smacking her when she got out of line, which was most of the time. "I was so loud." She still sounds like a five-alarm siren.

Life in the pimp's haven ended after three years, when her mom landed a man with a healthy income who added boatloads of clothes to Shannon's booty of stuffed toys. The good life rolled on for another year until the guy grew tired of funding her mother's heavy drug habit. He bailed out. Shannon's mom, smacked out to the point she could barely hook, began panhandling. She used Shannon as the draw. "I was so cute. People would give me money while my mom sat on the pavement smiling."

No daddy to help out, doesn't even know who he is. After she was born, he split and never returned. Shannon endured a few more years shuffling between her mother and grandmother. She looked in the mirror when she turned fourteen, saw the power of her skirt, and blasted out of Philly.

She found a boy with a car who drove her to California, unloaded him a couple of weeks after arriving in San Fran. She knew how to make money, but there was a glitch. "You can't do anything on your own when you're under eighteen, can't get an apartment, can't even buy a pack of fuckin' cigarettes. You gotta be with a pimp. You try it on your own, some other pimp will hurt you bad. It's not a choice."

On the stroll and underage, three or four pimps along the way while bouncing between S.F., L.A., Dallas, Vegas. She played the Lolita card, pulling down a hundred or more while the skanks on the corner would lowball for a Jackson. On her eighteenth birthday, bye-bye to Iceberg Slim, hello to escort services as an independent contractor. She's done well, always pays her rent on time, burns up the rest of the cash as fast as it comes in, and has enough clothes to fill the Union Square Gap five times over.

Tonight, she's wearing loose-flowing black pants, a Stormy Leather-style chain-link belt, and a dark red crop top exposing an inch of tight tummy. Soon as she gets in the car, she lights up a cigarette and unloads. "Christ, I don't know what to do. This is the second time my mom has ripped me off. Then she lies about it. Can you believe it?"

I cut to the chase. "When is she going back to Philly?"

"I don't know. When I ask, she gets all uppity and says 'I'll leave tomorrow if that's what you want.' That is what I want but . . . she makes me feel like I'm tossing her out to the dogs. I mean, she's been here over a month, and I think she's decided to park here for good. Doesn't pay any rent, eats all my food, trashes the living room. Only good thing is she sleeps about twenty hours a day, so I don't have to deal with her too much."

Shannon paid for her mom's Greyhound ticket to come visit for a couple of weeks. She hadn't counted on the round-trip turning into a one-way. Shannon manipulates men; her mother manipulates Shannon.

A cascading mane of silvery blonde hair swishes past her cheeks as she leans her head back, exhaling two thin trails of smoke through her nostrils. Her eyes close, her cell rings, she lazily holds it against her ear. "Whaz up . . . yeah, I'm comin' for sure, but I'm kinda busy right now . . . got any weed? Cool . . . okay . . ."

My cell rings. It's a fish on the line at the Argent Hotel whom I've been trying to hold; he's about to bail. "Wait a sec, Shannon's right here." I pass my phone over and mouth the word "cancel." In a flash, her cell falls away, and she's on mine, nauseatingly sweet-talking the man back into Zen. We crash down Market to the Argent, and an hour and a half later, we're climbing up a flight of steel stairs on the outside of a warehouse where Shannon will see her new boyfriend (the latest two-week fling bird-dogging her regular boyfriend), who's playing with a band at a private party (meaning word got around by e-mail).

The place is packed. I feel like Grandpa as I survey the crowd. I'm sure nobody who got that e-mail was over twenty-three. No stage. The three-piece old standard two-guitars-and-a-drum blasts away under a single spotlight. Shannon points to her latest acquisition, a tall, rail-thin bass player with the face of a crushed strawberry. A switch for her—Shannon's usually into beefy hip-hop boys. Pleases me thinking maybe thrash guitar still rules.

Strawberry's also the band's dubious vocalist, whose guttural hyperventilatings cling to the tattered banner of post-punk pandemonium. I can't make out any of the words except the refrain "fuck ice cream." Shannon's hand squeezes mine, and drags us through flaying bodies. Then she stops, stands rigid, shakes her shoulders for a minute, leans into my ear with "Gotta go do something" and sidles off.

I make my way back to the refreshment bar, five kegs (two bucks a paper cup) and cartons of Evian (three dollars a bottle) stacked against a brick wall. I point to the tower of water and pass a five to a guy wearing a Yale sweatshirt. He hands me an Evian, and I can't resist the Ivy League question. He answers: "Naw, I ripped it off from George W. Bush."

I saunter off, leaving him the change. My eye catches a long-legged pie in wine-red pum-pum shorts and do-it-to-me pumps dancing alone or maybe with six others. Used to imagine balling that kind of action, and now I'm saying under my breath, a babe like that could easily pull in big bucks for Zen. In this line of work, it's best not to taste the candy. Some of the girls are up for a run with the pimp; others won't even consider it. Those in the no-lip-twirling-on-Daddy camp like working for me, having worked for other services for about seventy-two hours, and then been told by the pimp that it's time for "an audition."

However, I'm not a total Zen monk. After I started Zen, I waited for the right girl to come along—Havana, a Latin firecracker I couldn't resist. We worked out a little side arrangement, and it still holds. When she arrived on the scene, I set up an appointment with one of my regulars who had paraded through the Zen roll call. Havana weaved her magic spell, and now he only wants to see her. I fully understand why. Problem is, she's max unreliable, always telling me she's ready to make a call, then changing her mind. Except for the regular, who's super rich and tosses her extra bucks. When Zen dolls mess me up like that, I just stop calling them. Unable to keep my thoughts off her face and my hands off her legs, I cut Havana a lot more slack.

In Pimpworld lingo, I "turned out" Havana. In fact, most escorts turn themselves out, usually around high school graduation or expulsion time. After giving two or three guys a turn in Albany, Duluth, or Tampa, the girl splits her hometown for the big money in the big city. And anonymity.

In San Francisco, she picks up a copy of *SF Weekly*, turns to the sex ads in the back pages, calls the Zen line listed in my two-inch classified. More than fifty applicants called the first time I ran the ad. Appointments at cafés. The résumé is built into the face and body, the way she struts her wonders, her ability to radiate a "yes" for the misplaced hopes and dreams of the john. Fat, trackmarks, missing teeth, or kids send the girl back out the door. (Some pimps will babysit; not this one.) Pluses for Zen: She's in the café when I arrive, she's wearing a tank top and tight pants. I need to see a tight tummy. She should know this. Smoker. Drinker. Doper, up to a point. Better if her boyfriend knows what's up. He can also drive her to her appointments. If she says she doesn't have a boyfriend, thumbs down: She's lying. All escorts have boyfriends except lesbians. Double plus for dykes. They make the best escorts, since there's no conflict of interest.

All the job candidates have made numerous false steps along the line. They are insecure and unstable, but this works in favor of pimp (daddy). A good sense of humor is helpful. Penetrating eye contact during the interview is crucial. One applicant looked at me for a moment, then turned her eyes away and talked to the window. A disaster if she did this with clients! She must have sensed my unease, stared into her coffee mug for a few moments, then gave me a long, meditative look and said, "I'm sorry. I'm having a hard time looking at you. You look so much like my ex-husband."

Maybe true, maybe a lie, but I hired her on the spot. Shortly before the interview concluded, the cell rang. I fumbled for it in my jacket pocket, handed it across the table. In a high-pitched, maybe slightly overbaked animated voice, she briefly described herself, then went directly to the close. Asked when he wanted to see her, not "Would you like to see me?"

She tapped the table, held up her thumb and forefinger in an O sign, bored in. "Tomorrow? . . . Sure, that'd be great . . . Valentine's Day, right, I almost forgot . . . sure, I'd love to be your Valentine" (sticks out her tongue, inserts finger in mouth, feigns vomiting) ". . . uh, I don't know about that, maybe a big ol' chocolate heart . . ."

Needing a breather from the thrash band, I step outside, snort another line of speed off the back of my hand. The air smells cool and fresh, with a slight scent of weed floating upward. Three guys huddled on the metal staircase below silently pass a joint. Across the street, a long, low building with shattered windows is decorated with jagged yellow bands of graffiti, unusually well-done by the low standard of San Francisco spray-painting crews, the painted blocks imitating and mocking the cracked glass.

I smoke a cigarette, then return to the ear-splitting rage. I weave through the crowd toward the band, looking for Shannon. Don't see her, focus on Strawberry slapping his guitar only a few yards in front of me. Once again, I hear "fuck ice cream." Briefly I wonder, what is his issue with ice cream? Torn jeans, no shirt, a set of military dog tags dangling on a gold chain around his neck, a boot-sized tattoo of an Iron Cross on his pasty white chest. Hitler tchochkes.

Everybody around me grinds and humps while clutching Evian bottles. An Asian boy wearing wraparound dark blue sunglasses flits past me with the pum-pummed $500 ticket, her sleek bod shimmying, her enormous lips puckered. Suddenly she seems to fade away, and all I see are dozens of pink labels zigzagging in the darkness overhead. I make a mental note to cut back on the speed, confine it to special occasions, much the same way I once rationed Snickers. This fleeting thought fuses with a plus: Speed reduces my alcohol intake to an occasional glass of red wine. No desire to hit the booze, and don't eat much either, although I need to start inhaling pounds of pasta to keep my 6'3" 175-pound frame from going skeletal.

Another bonus: Speed slam rolls my workouts at the 24 Hour Fitness down by the Embarcadero. Pressing, chinning, lifting, crunching abs, out the door into the fog, sprinting around Bank of America, legs pumping happy happy happy hot & sweaty through the cold air rolling off the dock by the bay.

Speed, ice, glass, crystal, shards, meth, zip, cat, crank—whatever it is my dealer retails, I'm certain I know what's in it, but don't want to know. He always assures me his product combines only the proper molecules off the periodic table, but his frequent resupply trips to Fresno make me think the chemist's lab is located at the dead end of an old stretch of blacktop. The cooker, having flipped through *Uncle Fester's Advanced Techniques of Clandestine Psychedelics & Amphetamine Manufacture,* stirs up his concoction with the only coat hanger in the Kozy Kottage's motel closet. His brew likely contains paint remover, Dektol photo developer, ephedrine, hydrochloric acid, and dead cats bubbling in a glass jug over a crusty hot plate.

Strawberry flops around like a spastic in a high school gym class. I'm transfixed by his dog tags flipping to and fro. Blackness descends around me. The amped-up decibels seem to merge with another sound, a sound seizing stronger on my mind, a distant sound, a sound leaping off an Asian wind. My eyeballs burn like light bulb sockets. Strawberry's dog tags grow larger, a whirling dervish closing in . . . vertigo.

I snap my head back and stare straight into the white spotlight above, but all I see are giant dog tags whirling like helicopter blades in the eye of a hurricane, hurling me back to the shooting gallery where I'm dropped on a landing zone along the Ho Chi Minh Trail. I scurry out of the LZ with the other Marines, trudge through a rice paddy flooded into an almost impassable swamp. Our boots slosh forward, plowing through muddy water up to our knees. *Ping, ping.* We charge forward toward a dike, the monsoon rains pushing against us. More rifle fire coming in, a half-second later a long low whistle from the hedgerow in the distance, *whoooosssh, whoooosssh.* Mortar shells burst twenty yards in front of us. A shower of shrapnel and mud cuts through the rain, then more mortars uproot the earth. Closing in on the dike, we hit the ground on our bellies, rattling like tin men loaded down with rifles, helmets, and flak jackets and strapped in cartridge belts strung with bayonets, ammo magazines, canteens of water, and canteens of Kool Aid. I'm flat on the ground clenching my teeth, dirty water in my eyes, hands plastered with mud. I dig into the earth, trying to bury myself under the dike. Machine gunners and riflemen return fire as bullets sweep over the dike. I hear a scream down the line but don't look up. *Fuck ice cream.* The mortar rounds stop. No more rifle fire in the distance. I look down the line and see a wounded grunt. I peek over the dike. I see the hedgerow, know only the shadowy forms of the Viet Cong lurk in the distance, melting into the monsoon rains, vanishing into the treetops. *Fuck ice cream.* Strawberry smiles at me. I bail out of the warehouse.

The first rays of dawn paint streaks of pink across the sky. I walk to my car, look around, still dazed and not quite sure where I am. I drive a few blocks over a maze of rusted railroad tracks cutting across an industrial wasteland, turn on 16th Street, and see the looping freeway band overhead, the early commuters zipping to work while my, uh, shift is done. A half-dozen boxy brown trucks lined up in front of the UPS outlet look like an Army caravan. A couple of husky drivers jauntily roll overflowing hand trucks down a ramp, the first wave of commerce firmly packaged and soon to be sold.

The streets are nearly empty. I stop at a light. A car pulls up beside me, stops for two seconds, then roars through the red light. I look around, hoping a cop car will appear out of nowhere, blast that siren up the dude's tailpipe.

No such luck. On Valencia a few men stationed idly in front of a dingy bar look pretty juiced up. Another guy approaches, and they huddle around him—probably a drug dealer with some morning wellness.

A few blocks down, I spot a *Chronicle* truck dumping off a stack of newspapers at a green-tubed kiosk manned by an aging cigar smoker. I pull over in a red zone. The newsstand guy sees me coming, snaps the cord on the stack with a pocketknife. A slight smile passes over his yellowed teeth as I hand him a quarter. The smell off his stogie mingles with the candied air in front of a Mexican bakery's open door—its pink and yellow sugary cakes stacked on a slanting tray in the window. I pass on the confectioner's powder barrel, spin downtown.

Slurping down coffee at the Pine Crest Diner on Geary, I'm giddy over the possible benefit from the Strawberry zapping. Post-Traumatic Stress Disorder at last! It's about time. What took so long? I may be at the back of the line, but this could be worth a few hundred bucks a month if I game it right at the VA.

Got the creds. Saw a fair amount of action. Then again, didn't leave a drop of blood over there, made sure to keep my ass down and cower behind trees, rice paddy dikes, or concrete bunkers left over from the Frenchmen's earlier campaign. Never put the rifle to my eye. I carried a .45 pistol and a camera. War was sweet and sour for those of us in the Third Marine Division photo lab. We were scattered all around, humping the boonies from the red hills outside of Chu Lai to the ancient Citadel in Hue, a brick-walled fortress which stretched into the distance along the banks of the River of Perfumes. We'd "snap the war," then return to the safety of the Headquarters Battalion near Da Nang and process our film.

Time seemed to stop in the darkroom as the war out in the field whirled on. A mixed bag of propaganda and the real war emerged from rolls of 35-millimeter film hanging on a line of string like dead snakes in a Bombay bazaar. Sheets of Kodak paper submerged in Dektol slowly collected a spectrum of whites, blacks, and grays. A silhouetted figure slapping a magazine in his rifle, a cigarette dangling from his mouth; a Navy Corpsman bandaging a wounded jarhead, his eyes rolled back, blood trickling out of his nose; a clean-shaven Marine, proud and stern, saluting an officer awarding him a Silver Star; a village child in tears, holding the pitiful remains of a burnt hoe in his hands.

The peculiar clashes between East and West always made good pictures. An old Vietnamese woman hung laundry on an artillery piece protected by a wall of sandbags and wheels of barbed wire. Beyond a tall stack of five hundred bags of rice bearing labels from Arkansas loomed acres of gracefully terraced rice paddies that melted into the distant hills beyond.

A *Life* magazine photographer captured an image of a little boy guiding a four-hundred-pound water buffalo through a field. Definitely a contented water buffalo, tuned into Armed Forces rock 'n' roll from a transistor radio hanging off one of his horns. Once, while taking pictures of sunshiny Marines constructing a school-house in a village outside of Hue, I panned my Nikon across the side of a pagoda. A strange sensation ran through me when the viewfinder filled up with the moon-sized eye of the Cao Dai etched in a triangle, peering back at me. I put my finger on the shutter, suddenly froze up, then started laughing. I spoke to the eye. "Okay, buster, which one of us is going to blink first?" No picture, but not really on my account. I'm sure my invasive finger was gently lifted off the shutter by the peaceful spirit from the City of Southern Kings.

The darkroom had a great perk: air-conditioning, a luxury reserved for the general's bunker atop a hill overlooking the base and a few other techno-compounds. The photo lab's cool box built into a truck held out the promise of returning home. In the sealed blackness, I could see the waves crashing over the rocks on the Oregon coast, fir trees bending in the wind on the campus at Eugene, the rain beating on the windows of my parents' house in Portland.

But this cool oasis was also a haven in a cruel carnival where twisted clowns toted shotguns through the valleys, and sleight-of-hand artists in the CIA carried out extreme measures. In the clouds above, lethal toys defoliating the landscape and wiping out entire hamlets didn't win over many Vietnamese hearts and minds. For that matter, precision bombs, smart bombs, cluster bombs, and Daisy Cutters didn't get the patriotic blood in me flowing. And yet, however counterproductive bombing might be, when you're in a foxhole under fire, the sight of an American jet whizzing overhead is lovely, and the sound of its payload sweet. You feel safer after the bombs hit, even if you're not.

Total war reeks of intoxicating beauty. Waves of milky-green uniformed men swallowing each other in elephant grass, plumes of black smoke from mortars rushing in a line across a rice paddy, furious streams of fire from a Phantom eating across the top of a tree line, massive tanks spinning their tracks on a muddy floor. Even more spectacular, the night war, a dreamscape of white flares swinging down gracefully in their tiny parachutes, orange tracer rounds slicing low across the sky, the moon spilling light on crunched figures along a ridgeline, the booming sound of artillery echoing through the valley.

The war machine also dishes out an undertow of violence that can't be covered up by an aesthetic overdose. War allows a guy to do pretty much anything he wants—no restraints, no taboos, no no's. And such a nice weapon, the M-16. Lightly squeeze off a round with the butterfly trigger, or switch it over to rock 'n' roll—automatic fire. This is not to say everybody behaved like the soldiers who slaughtered civilians in the village of My Lai, but the blurring of lines between combatants and noncombatants made it easier to shoot first and ask questions later.

Time spent dipped in combat was offset with many reprieves back in the darkroom. Along with hot showers behind a row of tents and hot food at the mess hall, we could kick back with American Budweisers and Vietnamese Beer 33 at the enlisted men's club. Occasionally, we'd sneak off to the warriors' cathedral of dreams, the Tiger Bar in Da Nang. One must go there. In the thunder of war an interlude at the Tiger might be the last stand.

On the second floor of a dilapidated building, the Tiger's creaky, drooping floor supported the weight of a platoon of Marines doing the bang-bang in a catacomb of cubicles constructed with two-by-fours and flattened cans of Bud. When crowded, the place trembled like S.F. during the '06 and '89 quakes, the seismographic couplings jacking up the Richter Scale.

As it happened, I only ventured in the bar once. Shortly after my arrival, all of downtown Da Nang was placed off limits. The girl I saw spoke about five words of English, and I the same in Vietnamese. But her mercurial eyes flashing copper, black, and green told a story she never told me, a story endlessly repeated under the Western flags in front of a column of boots marching into Vietnam.

I still see her eyes, big and round, yet flat. A child born of another war, a little girl who I'm certain grew up on the Streets Without Joy, the daughter of a French soldier she likely never knew. Then it was our turn. In her eyes I caught a glimpse of the legacy we would leave behind.

When the war finally ended, the mixed-race children's struggle for survival began. Neglected by Communist authorities because most of their mothers were prostitutes, and ostracized by many Vietnamese because they were "impure," they lived in the streets of the newly "liberated" Saigon, vilely renamed Ho Chi Minh City in honor of the butcher from the North. These kids with Anglo or African features could be found near the better hotels where they sold black-market Marlboros to Russian advisors and begged European diplomats for soap. They were called *bui doi*—"children of the dust."

Nobody knows how many offspring of GIs were born during the war. Western refugee agencies have given estimates ranging from twenty thousand to fifty thousand. For many years after the war, efforts by church groups and refugee agencies to allow immigration for them and their mothers were stifled by twin bureaucratic structures: the booming imperial one in D.C. and the catatonic red one in old Saigon. Improved diplomatic relations since the mid-eighties have allowed many of the Amerasians into this country.

In 1992, one mixed-race twenty-two-year-old woman who made it to these shores achieved an American dream, at least from this pimp's point of view: Angela Melini graced the foldout page in *Playboy*. In some of the more stringent feminist quarters, getting tapped as Playmate of the Month would not be viewed as a triumphal moment for the children of the dust. But, given that Hugh Hefner's monthly selections were pinned up on barracks walls all over South Vietnam, Angela's ascendance into the ranks of bunnies strikes me as a fitting end to the war, far better than those photos in 1975. Unlike the American Huey helicopters falling into the South China Sea, Angela's flotation devices had deployed.

A fat man spilling over his seat at the Pine Crest counter talks nonstop to himself, little stabs with a purple Crayola in his twitching fingers slash squiggly lines across the cover of the *SF Weekly*. I conclude the Strawberry moment is insufficient evidence for filing a PTSD claim. I have no problem pimping, but I won't rip off the VA. Most people pay several hundred dollars a month for health insurance; I get excellent health care at the VA for a pittance.

Crazy I am, running an escort service, living outside the law, snorting speed, chained to the ship of fools by my own choice. Will the Zen ship go down in a storm? I don't care. *Ride the storm.* If I do go down, the one thing I won't do is name names like Heidi Fleiss. The Hollywood procuress for the stars didn't just break the rules of the game by ratting out Charlie Sheen; she violated the game's categorical imperative.

My secret life as a pimp meshes nicely with my public persona: I'm a low-end journalist, a freelancer. I do write for the *San Francisco Chronicle*, really the newspaper's pet freelancer since my byline pops up on a semiregular basis, though never enough to suit me. Obviously, the editors on Fifth and Mission don't know I run an escort service.

Most reporters kick off their future careers writing for their high school papers. My first byline, an article on Hitler's sex life, appeared in *Screw* during a midlife crisis when my checkered career as a traveling book salesman teetered into Willy Loman territory. I quit before I got fired. I'd been writing off and on for many years— mostly off.

My major project during the not-really-writing years was the standard favorite of all who served: The Great American War Novel. Vietnam veterans have an edge here, since the big one—our *Naked and the Dead* or *Red Badge of Courage*—has yet to be written, though Tim, Thom, Gustav, and Stephen have penned contenders.

Mine remains in a cardboard box filled with manila folders. Not a manuscript, mind you, but pages of notes, pages of dialogue that go nowhere, timelines, outlines, many plots leading to no plots, character studies including that of Second Lieutenant Hamlet, whose head got shot off during the Tet offensive in Hue. But he lives on, his head replaced by a television set that barks out suicidal orders to his troops from Nixon in the White House. Like that, Oliver Stone? You can have it. I've packed it in on the war novel.

When my article on Hitler's sex life ran in *Screw*, a weekly compost of putrid stories—but funny, well-written putrid stories—I felt honored to be pulled out of the slush pile by the sex rag's psychopathic editor, Al Goldstein.

Eventually, I ended up in San Francisco working for *Exotic*, a slick monthly "tits and ass" magazine based in Portland that covers the sexual carnival in the Northwest. *Exotic*'s publisher, Frank Faillace, a thirty-two-year-old businessman who started the magazine by maxing out his credit card, decided to expand his empire with a Bay Area version. I happily alerted our lonely male readers to the wondrous masturbatory fodder encased in a glass cage at the Lusty Lady peepshow, the debauched goings on in Baghdad by the Bay's strip clubs, and the durability of bullet vibrators.

The SF version was a two-man op: ad salesman and editor. Nice to have the title "editor," although my main duty required distributing the free magazine to strip clubs, adult bookstores, and massage parlors along with dropping off the rag to a few legit bookstores, cafés, head shops, and indy record stores that allowed a sex rag amongst their heaps of alternative sludge.

I became one of the happy cogs in the sexual-industrial complex, contributing to the economic strength of the American Empire. Annual revenue: Between $30 and $50 billion for the combined income from hardcore DVDs, softcore pay-per-view adult films in hotel chains, strip bars, Internet websites, phone sex on chatlines, sex toys, T&A magazines, and dirty books.

Not bad, since none of this is real sex.

All of us who work in the sex industry are cut off from normal existence. We are remote from other people except our fellow pervs. Making my rounds dropping off bundles of *Exotic*, the bouncer outside the Crazy Horse on Market wonders if I might know anybody who could bankroll him to the tune of forty grand so he could open his own peeler bar. The guy breaking fives into rolls of quarters for patrons at the Lusty Lady peep-o-rama in North Beach lays out a plan to shoot a hip-hop porn vid. The clerk at J&B Adult Book Shop in the Tenderloin says he went to a swingers event at a mansion in Sausalito, where couples paid $50 at the door. He wants to buy a big house and make the payments by charging $300 for weekend marathons.

Most of the minimum-wage smut workers have a plan to strike out on their own, knowing the cash cow is right in front of their eyes. So did I. Alas, after two years, the SF *Exotic* folded. Having dealt with escorts coming in and out of the office to place ads, I knew what to do next. But running an escort service? The question drifted down slowly, and the answer kept coming up yes. Risky? Sure, but that gives life a lift. Illegal? Technically no, but everybody knows it's just a cover for prostitution. Stupid? For sure. I didn't care. The more I thought about it, the more I liked it. A calculated move, not a blind leap into the No Zone. All you need to start an escort service is one girl and a box of condoms.

Escorting and freelancing mesh easily. My position at the bottom of the journalistic food chain spurs on my overwrought ambitions. I am an essayist. I have the eye of a *tirailleur.* But all my long, thoughtful essays sent off to magazines that matter get SASE'd. This angers me. In my professional capacity as a freelancer of quirky compositions on a wide range of cultural questions, my sentences splash across my notebook like Louis M. Eilshemius's transcendent painting of the *Afternoon Wind*; at one and the same time, I advance my arguments with the rigorous precision found in the philosophical topography of Wittgenstein's *Tractatus.*

This conceit flares up when one of my stories runs in the *Chronicle.* I write for "Insight," the Sunday op-ed section. On those happy Sundays I always spend the entire morning in North Beach at Café Roma, fueled up on a triple espresso, and dream *The New Republic* will someday recognize the finely honed journalistic sensibilities of a fellow traveler. During my precious published hours, Café Roma overflows with young women scribbling in their journals, lawyers reading the *New York Times,* and a ruthless critique of American global hegemony by a regular faculty gathering huddled around three tables buttressed together. My eyes discreetly survey all the tables—in particular, any table where a discriminating reader absorbed in "Insight" is soaring into the empyreal realm.

Maybe another quirky composition will appear two weeks later, but more likely, a four-month drought without a byline. During the drought, I spiral downward until one afternoon I stumble out of sleep, read over a just-finished finely polished essay glowing off my Dell monitor, and conclude that I might as well stop writing because all I'm doing is dropping another turd on a Microsoft Word file of tedious shit.

The cell rings, and I'm off in the gold pile to pick up a Zen doll. Up yours, *TNR!*

To suggest the crushing force of rejection that all writers experience led me to pimping is absurd. I am well-schooled and could get a legit job. Nonetheless, rejection is a terrific motivator for leaping into the void where an "I don't give a shit" attitude rules. Working for *Exotic* opened the door where I discovered the darkest corner of the sex industry. Easy money and a taste for danger played into it. Not too much danger, though—just enough to keep my nerves popping, like Vietnam without Mr. Charles drawing a bead on me.

Running an escort service allows me to surround myself with women, while keeping safely detached. I enjoy being an intimate part of their lives, but not having to give too much in return. In the darkness of my room, listening dopily to NPR, I thrive on picking up the cell phone and closing a flesh sale. Nice, too, when a woman is nearby, my fix having always been a candy-coated temptress like Havana, with a shiny hard ass and strong silk legs.

Never married, no kids, can't commit. Insensitive, indiscriminate, irredeemable. Such an attitude reeks of age twenty. You can be an adult in every other way and remain a fixated adolescent when it comes to women. I respect men who get married, raise a family, choose a career around twelve and stay the course till they drop in the grave. Even more, I admire the bootlicking sycophants networking their way to the top rungs of corporate greed or political power. They represent the economic cement holding the American foundation solid, so that a few of us can remain isolated monads bouncing through life with few responsibilities, zero obligations, and lots of time on our hands to sit around cafés reading magazines.

Or pimping.

Better yet, practicing the politics of pimping.

My respect for order, authority, and tradition stem from necessity: a check on my fondness for turning everything upside-down. This always requires the spilling of blood. Even if wrong, it seemed so right when a deranged mob, whipped up in a fevered state, stormed the Bastille, the Winter Palace, the Pentagon. You don't have to think, just act. At last, we can all be bad apples! Cops toss tear gas canisters into the crowd, anarchists pick 'em up and toss them back at the cops. Shit flies in every direction. Sirens wail. Nobody knows what's going down or what will happen next, and the only real objective is to break on through to the other side. "What's over there?" "Who cares? *Git it.*"

A case in point: an image on the tube from some street insurrection in '68 or '69. Paris? Prague? Berlin? Mexico City? I don't recall where, but I well remember watching the riot, the camera panning the crowd, then zooming in and lingering on the flames gutting a car. When I saw the flames licking across the car's windshield, *my dick got hard.*

So it is satisfying knowing that this is my last chance to chip away at the bourgeois social order, even if nowadays I can barely get it up, with or without a televised riot. Winks. Secrets. Pretending. Hypocrisy. I cherish and hold fast to these small vices. A million escorts on a million nights flame through the world, but really, I swear, nothing happened.

Is prostitution nothing more than the annihilation of the soul? If so, then I'm the guy in charge of the morgue. What about the hard and sad truth from Shannon: *"What can I do? I can't throw her out. I love my mom."*

A few days after hearing her say that, I saw a story in the *Chron* underscoring a new family trend: parents frustrated by their "kids" in their twenties who move back home after graduating from college. The right job befitting their status hasn't come along. These slackers, sucking on the suburban tit, are not outcasts. Shannon, supporting her mom, remains one because she fucks for money.

Only, unlike Mom and Dad, I keep a percentage of my kids' take.

THREE

Havana's wine-dark skin is consumed in flames. She twirls around over me, sticks her right thumb in her thong, bumps her hip, deftly stretches out her long golden arms above her head, and freezes in position, her body like a marble statue immune to the fire. Stomach taut as a steel band, nostrils flared, a smirk on her face. Dark, dangerous eyes—ignited.

Lying on the floor, my ear two inches from a speaker blasting out an infernal drum and bass mix, I reach toward her, slip a C-note into the flames. I feel nothing. The flames leap across my bookshelves, lick the high windows, and sizzle across the carpet. Havana's frozen stance undulates into a wild, primitive frenzy. Like an unabatable animal, the Latina firecracker charges around the room, her long snaky black locks shaking against the blaring beat of the music, the compact brilliance of her slender body illuminated by the fire of about two dozen candles scattered about the room.

I'll never drop E again.

After quizzing me on the inventory of drugs I'd consumed in the age of Led Zeppelin, Havana had plunked a tab of Ecstasy in my mouth. Seems like a cross between speed, acid, and the atomic bomb. Now she wants to know if my first hit did the trick. "Feeling the E?" she shouts over the music.

"Quite a mind rip, but I think I'll leave it to the ravers. And I need to soften the blow." I stand up, don't move for a moment until equilibrium falls back into my brain, replace her CD with Herbie Hancock, and turn the volume down by half. Havana plops down on the futon. "Okay if I take a nap?"

I drop my gaze, lick my upper lip. "Beauty rest is essential for a face that should be on the cover of *Vogue*."

She glances up, blows me a kiss. "I tried modeling once when I was in high school. The agency said I looked too ethnic. I said, hey, 'I'm half white, half Cuban.' Didn't matter, too dark."

"That's strange—fashion's big on mixed race."

"I think the lady I talked to didn't like me. I was late for the appointment, and she made a big deal out of that."

"That clears things up," I say pointedly, but she either misses or more likely chooses to evade the hint at her indifference toward promptness.

The half-nude half señorita blinks hard. "Lotta people mistake me for Asian. Or they ask, what are you? What the fuck difference does it make? I'm cute."

"You're a narcissist."

She opens her mouth to speak, hesitates, then mumbles the word under her breath. As she turns her head to the side for a moment, I sense she's stricken by this judgment. "A couple people have called me that, sort of in a joking way. So, uh, I'm not sure what it means. Like I'm arrogant?"

"Not exactly. You look in the mirror a lot, right?"

"Yeah, lots. Want to make sure I look good."

"But you already know you look good. So why bother?"

"'Cause I *like* looking at myself. I like being the center of attention."

"Exactly. That's a narcissist."

She claps her hands. "Cool. Now I know what I am. I like being a narcissist, and I do need my beauty rest," she concludes as her body slips under the billowing of a white comforter.

I step over to the window, tug it open from the bottom, lean out and inhale the cool night air. I operate my criminal enterprise out of an office in the heart of the city, the Grant Building on the corner of 7th and Market. The air smells fresh and clean. The street sweeper has lumbered through as it does every other night, swallowing up the preceding forty-eight hours of litter, crud, and waste. It won't take long for the fresh wet pavement to collect a mountain of candy wrappers, lakes of jelly doughnut goo, french fried fat driplets, Whammies, Eskimo pies, and ten thousand wads of chewing gum.

On the clean sheet of pavement below, a man appears, tosses a crumpled paper bag over the top of a trashcan. The cycle starts anew, but at least he tried. Another man from the shopping cart brigade parks his home across the street in the entrance to the Odd Fellows Hall. He takes some cardboard walls off the top of his overflowing cart, creates a temporary structure for the night, and disappears underneath.

A guardian of the Ninth District Circuit Court of Appeals, across the alley from the Grant, moves into view. A federal police car. The white fed cruises slowly down the block, the quiet hush of tires adding the right note of silence to the hour. No sirens from the firetrucks, no rattle of the streetcars, no drunken screams, nobody OD'd off the goods from the dealer bumpin' coke in the alley.

I turn away from the window and look over at the white comforter covering Havana. I see a cloud of white roses before my eyes and wonder: Is it the wind bringing freshness into these sultry hours, or might it be her? She can sink deep into dreams in about five seconds. What is behind her closed eyes? Am I in her dreams? I light a Camel Wide and sit down on the floor. The haze of cigarette smoke rolls around her magic circle of flickering candles. My eyes stare into the flames, hoping but failing to achieve harmony, enlightenment, truth, love, and joy.

When the Zen hour approaches, I snuff out the candles and wake Beauty, whose seductive hand is wrapped around a pink cell phone. "Good, won't lose it that way," I say, a small jab at her in light of two cells missing in action in the space of six weeks.

Proud of her minimalism, Havana frequently lashes out at people who accumulate lots of stuff. At the same time, she is forever losing keys, cigarettes, cell phones, notepads, rings, photographs (of

Havana), Rolling Writer pens (mine), hairbrushes, skin cream, lip-gloss, and a host of delicate powders.

I open a couple of beers, hand her one. She varnishes her toenails pink, then digs around in her purse and hauls out her makeup arsenal that no longer contains the weapons of penciled eyebrows and purple-black lipstick. When told the trashy trailer park slut-from-Hell aura blocks out the Zen waves, she agreed to a more "natural" look, but only under the condition I accept her counterproposal.

The scalp massage on my gray head was soothing, and I'm coming to terms with the instant return of ash brown hair. How-ever, I blew the negotiation by not including a demand that she never buy another fucking wig; the latest, which she is adjusting on her head, resembles a Parisian royalist's hairpiece plucked from the basket under the guillotine. She pokes around, weaves it into her own hair, the first phase of the Reign of Terror sticking out on both sides of her head like elephant ears.

I look straight at her. She sees below my boyish brown waves a face writhing in agony. Before I can speak, I hear, "I don't care what you think, I like big hair."

An opening for much ridicule, but I opt for silence, believing over time her wigs will fall into the dustbin of history along with gangsta rap and North Korea's Kim Jong Il. (With his people in the grip of famine, portly Kim has allegedly been washing down shrimp and kimchi with cognac, watching Daffy Duck cartoons, and giving lots of face time to a bevy of young women known as the "Pleasure Squad." This information, widely circulated by the South Korean CIA, could be disinformation. Then again, why bother being a dictator if you're not going to indulge in gluttony and debauch a squad of girls?)

I make a few phone calls while Havana dresses, tight black pants, black sandals, maroon silk top cut not too low, and a choke with a butterfly encased in cherry wood. "This is gonna be weird. You're sure this guy really doesn't want to fuck? He just wants me to piss on him?"

"Right, had one other guy call for a golden shower a few months ago. The girl said it was real easy."

"That's for sure, I'm looking forward to this. Better load up," she says, chugging down the rest of her beer. "Do guys call wanting to piss on girls?"

"None so far, and Zen would not accept a client who wishes to pee on poetry. Only the other way around."

"Hey, I like that—peeing poetry."

"Not quite. *You* are the poem on top of the guy satisfying his deviant need with a great release." I scan a tiny section on my book-shelf, spot a title so perfect I damn near have a great release myself: down comes Lawrence Ferlinghetti's *How to Paint Sunlight.* I read her a few lines.

I asked a hundred painters and a hundred poets
how to paint sunlight
on the face of life

"So you see, you're painting sunlight on his face. Christ, Ferlinghetti would cut my tongue out if he heard that."

Havana looks puzzled, maybe hurt. "Why? That's great, like I'm helping the guy, doing something good, not kinky or dirty."

"Hey, pop over to City Lights and tell Ferlinghetti. If he really wants to know how to paint sunlight, he's gotta ask the hookers, not just the poets and painters." My eyes move down the page, spot a zinger. Jabbing my finger on the line, I hold the book in front of her eyes. "And check this out: '*paint yourself as you see yourself / without make-up.*'"

She folds her arms, cocks her head. "I don't cake it on like I used to."

I turn my back on her. "That's true, and actually, it looks great, the light touch." I swivel around fast, with a peacock feather in my hand. "Take this with you."

"Ooh, this is really cool," she says covetously. "Can I have it?"

"Yes, and you'll need it soon."

She crunches up her face. "Like piss on the feather?"

"No, put it in your bag. You'll know when to use it." She runs her fingers lightly across the feather, says no more, and we're out the door rocketing into the night.

The gold pile rattles into the Tenderloin. Turning the corner on Taylor and Ellis, Havana points to the Glide Memorial Church, a refuge for the hordes of homeless in the city. "I can't believe I actually ate there a few times," she says.

"You're kidding."

"It was when I first moved to San Francisco, right after high school. And I lived with this guy, just a couple blocks away from here. He was sort of a gangster, Pablo, my last Hispanic guy. I like white guys now. *Only* white guys. Pablo was kind of exciting, a great dancer, but fucking lazy. I wanted to be a stripper and got a job right away at the Crazy Horse. Paid the rent while Pablo sat around watching boxing matches on TV. The money was good at Crazy Horse sometimes, then it would sorta dry up. We'd be broke and—"

"*You'd* be broke."

"Yeah, flat broke. And hungry. So we'd go to Glide. First thing I noticed is everybody working it. Be in line, and all you hear is how to get SSI and housing and food stamps. That's so wrong. Sitting on their butts all day while I'm dancing my ass off till two in the morning"—she pauses, adds in a soft tone—"but I did it too."

"Briefly, in a bind, nothing wrong with that." The blocks sweep by. I stop in front of an apartment building, speed dial for a pony in my stable. "Bianca's coming with us."

"Bianca? Didn't you say we'd be picking up Cordelia?"

"Yes, but she had to cancel. Full moon just struck."

"Too bad, that Bianca's a fucking bitch. Wish she was on her period."

The two girls have met only once whereupon Havana listened intently to Bianca's lengthy dissertation on her ability to manipulate men based on her degree in psychology from UCLA, after which she pointedly asked Havana if she'd gone to college. To her credit, Havana said no, rather than mentioning her one highly undistinguished semester at a community college.

"I think she was putting me down," Havana had told me while

Dr. Bianca was busy comforting her patient with oral gratification at the hot tub chamber on Van Ness.

Bianca's hoity-toity put-down on her first meeting with Havana, along with the fact that there's not a single book in her apartment, tells me the closest she ever got to UCLA was a well-paid basement gang-bang at a frat-house initiation ceremony, possibly amidst a flock of sheep.

Bianca is going with the new upgrading trend in the sex industry. A stripper can't be just a stripper any more. She's a painter who strips, or more likely a photographer, or more likely still, film director with a camcorder. A *Chronicle* story on dancers at the Lusty Lady confirms this: "They say some have doctoral degrees; some are in graduate school. One dancer is a lawyer."

They say.

That's the real story, but I'll go with the flow. A poet passed through Zen, yet her strong rebuff of several requests for a look-see compels me to question her output. (Still, maybe deep down in her soul lurks a Sylvia Plath, and I fear that if the muse strikes, the poem will be titled "PIMP Daddy.")

Escort services frequently advertise under names like College Girls, College Playmates, College Centerfolds, and Sorority Sweethearts. Although some women do combine study hall with balling for dollars, for the most part escorts don't spend a lot of time at the library. A lot of guys want a girl to come over dressed as a high school cheerleader, but very few ask for college graduates. They are not paying $500 for Havana's insight on the layers of meaning in a Jonathan Franzen novel; they want sex, not a term paper on *The Corrections.*

Bianca pops in the back seat, pulls a chocolate glazed doughnut out of a bag, and offers it to Havana, who takes one bite of it, then holds up the offering for me. I sneer, pull into the traffic. Bianca's languorous dark eyes burn in the rearview mirror, her short boyish haircut gleams with strands of yellow, blue, and a hint of red. "Bob hates doughnuts," she chirps.

"A million a month for Rolaids," I say. "Hey, Bianca, maybe you can help us out psych-wise on Fred, this guy Havana's gonna see. No sex, Fred wants her to stick a feather up his ass. Then he hops around the room shouting 'cock-a-doodle-doo.' What's up with Fred?"

Bianca lurches forward. "Now that's freaky, super freak. No sex, huh? Some guys like a dildo up the ass, but a feather? Hey, maybe we should switch calls. This sounds like a guy I can handle."

My favorite Zen doll nails Bianca. Out comes the peacock feather, fanning to and fro off her hand. Havana looks straight ahead and speaks to the backseat. "I can handle it."

I press on. "So Fred's freaky. But here's the thing I don't get, Bianca. Explain what a feather up the ass and crowing like a rooster means. Is there something in the guy's background, something that happened to him when he was a kid that causes him to crow? Is it deviant behavior like guys who want their eyeballs licked, or bee stings on their balls, or being mummified?"

Bianca sighs with a know-it-all air. "It means he's got his special thing. Everybody does."

Havana turns her head. "So is he maybe a narcissist?"

I cringe, quickly ask: "When you say you can handle Fred, you mean you'll help him temper his wildness so he will stop hopping about like a rooster? Do you want to try and cure his behavior so he will no longer have to bear this terrible burden?"

"Oh, no, you never try to change them. Just nod your head and smile and say 'what would you like?'"

So much for tackling the rooster question head-on. I lift my right hand off the steering wheel, jerk my thumb toward the passenger side. "I see. Well, Havana can do that without the benefit of psychology, don't you think?"

"Oh sure, whatever."

Havana looking straight ahead again. "Thank you."

Bianca touches my big-haired Latina on her shoulder. "I'm sorry, I got all excited by the feather thing. I wasn't trying to steal your call."

Havana twists clear around, leans over the seat, and hugs Bianca. "Oh, I wasn't thinking that at all. I know you meant well." They babble and laugh in sisterly solidarity as I turn on Market, running a few minutes ahead of schedule for the peculiar play about to commence in the glorious sepulchered ruins of the Sheraton Palace.

At a red light, a crusty down-and-outer at his post on the Muni bus island staggers forward, outstretched hand waving the *Street Sheet* four inches from my open window. San Francisco gathers the panhandlers from across the nation into its golden arms, offering them a decent package of benefits, including monthly cash grants, although a shit-disturber liberal city supervisor Gavin Newsom, despised by progressives, is trying to cut off the money supply. The *Street Sheet* is filled with stories trashing Newsom, and recounting the horrors of the domicile-challenged people anchored at the bottom of the ruthless capitalist mode of production.

I wave the wino away with an encouraging word. "Work the tourists in Union Square."

He persists. "C'mon, how 'bout a quarter?"

"Can't do it."

A dollar bill between two fingers slides behind my neck and out the front window. "I'll take a paper."

I want to amputate Bianca's tongue. The wino knows he has me right where he wants me, trapped at a red light. His jaundiced lips curl back in a mean triumphant grin. His stink shoots straight up my nostrils as he leans in the window, intentionally brushing the *Street Sheet* over my shoulder in what I must concede is a smooth hit job. No doubt he has paid over and over for his suffering, so the small victory of sticking it to the dude who refuses to part with spare change must be deeply satisfying—and handing the newspaper to Bianca no doubt doubly satisfying. He looks past me into the backseat, smacks his lips over a few remaining cracked teeth and says, "You are the most beautiful woman I've ever seen."

"Thank you, get a cup of coffee." I hear the crinkling of a paper bag, see it going past my neck. She adds to his booty. "Here's two doughnuts."

The bag is received, opened, a peek inside. "Chocolate glaze, my favorite. Yours too, I bet. Did you know the hole in a doughnut can be the same—"

"Uh, excuse me, green light." I ease slowly forward into the intersection, not wanting to give the stinking cunt a victory by tromping on the gas. I want to reach back and smash my fist in her face. I bite my lip, glance over at Havana, and sense her plans for Bianca are far worse than mine. Havana's eyes are black balls of fire, the true face of the Reign of Terror at its zenith, a face hurling a threat at giver, receiver, and anyone else in range; a threat along the lines of Figaro Beaumarchais: "If they are hungry, let them browse grass" as a temporary reprieve until the time is ripe for the only solution: "France must be mowed."

Bianca's client has checked into the Renaissance Parc 55 near the cable car turntable stop at Market and Powell, tourist central where visitors are welcomed by the city's ambassadors shaking Styrofoam cups.

I pull across the streetcar tracks to the curb. A taxi horn blares behind me. I flip him the bird and tell Bianca it might be more than an hour before I can pick her up. She says her boyfriend will taxi. "He's going to come get me, and then we're going down to San Jose to see some friends. So can I give you your cut tomorrow?"

"Sure," I say. She's off. Now, conference time with Havana's furious head, yelling, "You better call her right now and tell her you need the money tonight. She'll rip you off."

"No, she won't. I don't get the money, she doesn't get any more calls."

"I wouldn't trust her for a minute. That shit back there? You tell the fucking asshole 'no,' she says 'fuck you, Bob, fuck you up the ass.' No fucking respect—"

"You said you wanted to stop saying 'fuck' all the time."

Shrieking at five-alarm: "I do, but I'm fucking mad. I hate her. You know girls are *worse* than guys. Evil, she's pure evil." Havana draws her finger across her jugular vein. "Bounce that bitch."

"Calm down, baby, you're breaking my eardrum. I can't stand her either. But this is like any other business. She does a good job, she's always reliable, *always*, unlike some other girls in Zen I know"— I pause, raise an eyebrow in her direction. "The guys like her. She stays. And her haircut. Absolutely right. Would look great on *you*. Don't let her shit roll over you."

The last block holds nothing but silence, her lips tight in the shadow of the car. The gold pile pulls up behind a Lincoln Town Car in front of the Palace. "Focus on what's up, time to paint sunlight," I say softly, putting my hand on her leg, just above the knee.

And her face turns all sunlight. She opens the door, starts to get out, glances over her shoulder at me. "Wait. The feather up his ass, that's just a joke, right?"

I smile big. "Yes, and a failed psychology test. Take the feather with you, though—maybe Fred'd like his nose tickled during the flow."

"Okay, I'll ask him, or maybe I'll just whip it out for a surprise." Then she's gone, a flash of long legs strutting past the doorman.

I park a couple of blocks away, and walk back. Upscale hotel lobbies overflowing with stuffed chairs beside walnut desks always offer me a quiet place to read, while in a suite above, the ripe aroma of a Zen doll stokes desire. I feel as much at home in the Palace lobby as a financial consultant in his SOMA loft. My steps echo across the deserted marble floor, my secret life safe within the ornate gilded walls of discretion. I stroll past the Garden Court, peek in at the highly polished columns soaring toward a luminous stained-glass ceiling.

The Palace retains an air of aristocratic gentility, its dining room favored by the rich and powerful since it opened in 1909. President William Howard Taft was an occasional guest, scarfing down pressed duck on gilt-edged china. Questionable women who visited the Palace in those days were procured from a pimp sitting at his table by the steam piano at the Barbary Coast's Eye Wink Saloon, an opportunity for his dime-a-dance girls to pick up a good deal more than chump change.

I walk back down the hall into the enormous lobby. A bellhop stands by the entrance, arms folded, head erect. A clerk behind the counter gives me a quick glance, then looks down at some paperwork. My dress code is quite suitable for the Palace, a big change from the past.

One day I told Havana: "Maybe I should burn up some money on new clothes." She grabbed my arm, and in a flash a clerk at Versace on Post Street was bagging three pairs of flat-fronted black pants. Off to Armani, where she selected a sharp wool sports coat, over to Macy's for T-shirts, across Union Square to Saks for the final call on my credit card—a pair of tight burgundy pants seemingly made to order for her killer ass.

She suggested new wingtip shoes, but I stuck with my Serious

Tactical boots from Stompers, worn mainly by cops and beefy gay boys. Later, on my own, I impressed her with Liste Rouge custom-made shirts shipped in from Paris. Solid tan and light blue shirts with Palazzi cuffs. No monogram. Too stuffy for San Francisco.

Slouching down in a chair under the soft rays of the Palace's leaded crystal chandeliers, I try to understand a man's need for a golden shower.

I imagine Havana flashing a wide smile, sending a fat stream cascading in great arcs across the nude body of Fred. Her sultry voice sings, "You like that, I know you do," as she shifts her aim down his chest, along his legs, the steaming shower gushing like an endless rain, an infinite flow dissolving the physical boundaries, the limitless secretions from her moist depths sending Fred into delirium. Havana swims in the divine song, drenching Fred in her dew from the swamp behind her sugar walls. *Whizz, whiz, whizzzzz* go the pungent lines of gold, glimmering like the scribblings of sunlight from an old bongo-bongo red bridge poet's pen, his notebook pressed against the Tower of Finance on Montgomery Street. Havana reaches for a bottle of Bordeaux, holds it by the neck and tips it to her proletarian lips. "Resupply," she sings. Holding the bottle over her head, the wine spills through her hair, down her small alert breasts, through the canyon of cleavage, forming a purple pool below Fred's big heart. Wiggling over the body of capital, she again unleashes her power drawn from the guerilla spirit of her grandmother, whose battle cry from 1959 still echoes over the Sierra Maestra mountains of Cuba. The final fury, Zenista pissing on Batista.

Fred opens another bottle of Bordeaux after Havana slips out the door. He drops into a chair in front of Gates's Windows, yawns as a stream of sales numbers float across the blue screen, an essential element in his yet unprepared annual vision statement.

He scrolls into another number stream, his favorite, the corporate expense account. He closes his eyes and feels Havana's peaceful flow, smiles over the bonus peacock feather stroking his nose, even better the grand finale when she scooted forward and smashed her pink peach over his parched lips. He punches in $134 for the lunch meeting with his client; he'll amortize the remaining balance from the $500 Zen ticket onto future lunch nonmeetings.

Is Fred kinky? Well, small kinky, harmless, and I haven't a clue why this turns him on. Kinky requests, however fascinating, are few and far between. Most men simply want to get laid. Either they never could or no longer can score regular pussy. They are from every corner of the world and all walks of life. Cunny-hunting accountants from Omaha, peccatiphobic preachers from Pocatello, gassy morticians from Kalamazoo, bundles of corruption from DC, button-down bean counters from NYC, souvlaki importers from Istanbul, logical positivists from Vienna, Arab potentates, Japanese sword salesmen, and Eurotrash.

The planes swoop down on SFO, the men rush for cabs, and the stampede is on, a crop of cocks longing for Lucy Lunchmeat. One nibbles on Shannon in the back office under fluorescent lights, another pokes Cordelia for a nooner at the Mark Twain, a third strokes Havana on a deck overlooking the Bay, while the wife is in Norway seeking an au pair.

Some men want a slightly dangerous encounter. The stolen, the forbidden, the illicit, the whispered proposition excites them as much as the sex. The man knows nothing about the Zen doll who will soon arrive and throw him a fuck. And sometimes: "I didn't plan it, just a spur-of-the-moment thing, my God, I don't know what got into me." Like Hugh Grant in a white BMW with Divine Brown on Sunset Boulevard. Clearly, a hazard for the Brit in his cream britches out on a tear. He must have known the risk was high and clearly craved it, otherwise he would have found better digs for his moment with a prossie.

Unlike Grant, who could have almost any woman he wanted, most men who fall into a hooker's arms are socially inept. Oregon's former senator, Bob Packwood, unfairly sacked by his colleagues for his crude tongue-darting transgressions, said it best: "Some men are suave as Cary Grant and others have the motor skills of Quasimodo." Packwood should have *frequently* bit his tongue and called an escort service. So too President Bill Clinton. I still admire him, but what was he thinking in that Little Rock hotel room when he dropped trou in front of a startled Paula Jones?

Wait, I know. Big hair.

Escort services emphasize fantasy in their ads, but this is a transparent cover for what is really being sold. Strippers talk of "giving men a fantasy," which sounds better than lap dancing. Phone sex lines lay it on straight, since they only provide voice sex: "Slide Your Meat Between My Tits And Shoot Your Cum On My Face," or "Chinese Buffet—All You Can Eat."

In the sex biz, *fantasy* is another word for getting off. The most intriguing fantasies involve recreating peak moments of the past. In a man's circle of agitation and satiation, a woman from long ago always commands the center. Men call Zen looking for a replay with a girl who looks like a former flame. He'll have one of his ex's dresses at his house for Havana to wear, or her brand of perfume. He'll slip in his favorite CD, the one with an old song that pulls his old girlfriend's face out of the past.

One man told me of a woman he met ten years ago after following her for several blocks when they got off the same bus. He caught up with her, struck up a conversation. They went out. A one-night stand, his first, but apparently not hers. She didn't want to see him again. He harbored no hard feelings, just wanted it recreated. At the appointed hour, Cordelia got on the bus, went through the motions, and spent an hour with him at a hotel.

A retired widower said it was common practice after World War II for "stenographers" who did not know shorthand to meet men in hotels for dictation. One Zen doll gave him a real treat. She had a friend who worked in a retro clothing store, so she showed up in a '40s style dress, wide-brimmed hat, pencil, and notepad. (I wanted to top it off by having her sport a Dewey or Truman button, but couldn't find one on short notice.)

It boils down to this: a woman must draw upon all her strengths and a pack of lies to do this job. Cordelia pretends to be fire while her heart remains cool. All men are blind in the presence of a Zen nightbird; her eyes are spared nothing. The john is Anyman.

Anyman wants it anytime, anywhere. In a bed, on the staircase, against the wall, over the hood of a car, under the stars. But he usually wants more than a sex machine. He wants the rhythm and flavor of the real item. Mr. Baltimore, face-to-face with Cordelia, wants to understand her flesh. Here he is, his colossal erection ready to fire, his painful longings about to be swept away in the carnal juices of Venus, and he wants to make sure the *vibes* are right.

But on the Zen ship, the two clocks are never in sync. For him, the hour whips by too fast. For her, it's an endless sixty minutes of plowings and churnings. One nineteenth-century courtesan kept a record of how many thrusts her clients took before climaxing. On average, forty-five, she gloomily noted, "excluding hot-blooded young men, and lewd, experienced philosophical lovers."

At its most extreme, an escort's attitude toward men resembles Valeria Solanas's extermination program put forth in the SCUM Manifesto. The leading light, and perhaps only member, of the Society for Cutting Up Men, Solanas is best known for shooting Andy Warhol in 1968. SCUM advocated "eliminating" men, or at least making sure "Big Daddy is in the corner shitting in his forceful, dynamic pants."

But escorts don't want to kill off their source of income. They view men with studied indifference befitting older women.

An old sexist one-liner: Men pay escorts to leave.

Yes, but others want a never-ending hour. Take the case of James Boswell, who did not want his "delicacy" stained in the "gross voluptuousness of the stews." Worried about eighteenth-century STDs, he avoided the "nymph with white-thread stockings who tramps along the Strand," opted instead for an actress he calls Louisa at the Covent Garden theatre.

In his *London Journal*, Boswell admitted he fell for Louisa on their first date, and immediately expressed his deep affection for her. Louisa told him he was moving too fast. She agreed to see him again, on the condition he put his "preface" in the middle of the book.

On their second date, she yielded a bit, informing Boswell she was not a Platonist. ("This hint gave me courage.") A few days later, over breakfast, her insolence startled Boswell. She confessed her bad mood stemmed from a "trifling debt" expected to be paid in six weeks. How much? he inquired. Two guineas. He gave her the money, adding that was all he had, and she said she would pay it back.

Forced to get by on cheese for a while, Boswell consoled himself, noting "I suffered in the service of my Mistress." On their next date, another rebuff of the preface. Depressed, he gave Louisa some more money and she told him if he was "of the same opinion" in a week she would make him "blessed."

He sold his suit, a lace hat, and a penknife to get through the long week. By now, Boswell was so horny he could have ravished an entire boarding school, but he cooled his desire over tea and snuff until the appointed hour. He walked to the flat where the Hanging Sleeve Lady allowed him to lay sheets across a featherbed. This gave him the impression that a baptism in the Science of Copulation would soon commence. She embraced him, dangled the carrot with a "sweet elevation of a charming petticoat," but held him in line with the excuse that the landlady hovered nearby. She'll be in church tomorrow, Louisa assured him, return then.

He did, and she kept her word. But just as he was about to make a "triumphal entry," the couple heard the God-fearing steps of the landlady. "We were stopped most suddenly and cruelly from the frutation of each other." The next day "nature's periodic effect" intervened. Finally, after nature had taken its course, James and Louisa got it on. "Five times I was fairly lost in the supreme rapture."

As it turned out, Louisa's rapture carried with it the same fear Boswell had assigned to the tramp on the Strand—a dose of the clap. Boswell couldn't believe Louisa was so "sadly defiled" until the doctor told him of the "poisonous infection." His delicacy did not prevent him from confronting Louisa and asking for his money back. She denied the accusation, kept the money, and dumped him.

Kafka's case is quite different. From a hooker's point of view, Kafka was a douchebag. In a liaison with a shopgirl who turned an occasional trick, Kafka lost his virginity at age twenty. Afterwards, bumping into her in the streets of Prague, he pretended she was a stranger. He could not stand the sight of the shopgirl who had made repulsive remarks and used obscenities. This weighed on him for many years. He found sex disgusting, so at one point, when his infatuation with a married woman got the best of him, he imagined he had metamorphosed into a beetle. He only wanted to run across the carpet of the couple's "great household" once a year. It would be a terrible loss for literature had Kafka not sublimated his sexual desires by churning out stories.

He knew how to play that bug.

FOUR

S weet scents waft up from cinnamon rolls, apple dumplings, muffins, and biscuits on the counter at Café DeLucchi in North Beach. I check out the menu. "I'm famished. Didn't eat much yesterday."

"It's the speed," says Havana. "Bad shit."

"What about E?"

"A party trip, not a death trip."

"Right," I snort. The Mediterranean omelet appeals except for the red onion, dangerous to my delicate stomach.

Havana scrutinizes the bakery items, leaning a little too close. "Hmm, one of those biscuits will do it for me."

"They're great, that's what I usually get. Maybe I'll just have a couple of biscuits."

"Don't let me stop you. Have breakfast."

I look at the menu again. "I can't make up my mind."

"You never can."

"Not true." The waiter sets a teapot and double espresso on a tray. "We'll have three biscuits." He nods, squeezes them onto the tray. "See how decisive that was," I brag, jauntily carrying the tray to a table by the corner window.

"If I hadn't said anything, you'd have taken all day trying to figure out what to eat. Everything with you is maybe, sometimes, perhaps, perhaps, perhaps. You seem so"—she searches for the right word—"both ways."

I shake my head. "Not really, it's a matter of looking at a variety of views. Reality is gray, like that teapot."

She picks up her spoon and clanks it on the pot. "This is silver, not gray."

"Perhaps," I say, taking a big bite out of a biscuit.

She rolls her eyes. "Silver, no doubt about it. I mean the color silver, not real silver."

"Hold on there, Ms. Certainty. Assume the teapot is real silver. Then is it silver-colored?"

"That's a stupid question."

"Think so, huh? Stupid or no, answer it."

"Yeah, 'course it's a silver color if it's silver."

I finish the biscuit and start on another, thinking maybe I should have ordered breakfast. "Hmm, these are good. So wouldn't you agree that the only true silver color is in any object that's made of silver, like a silver spoon or a silver coin?"

"That's even more stupid. Lots of things have a silver color."

"I said true silver color. If the object is not made of real silver, then the color is mock silver, or *perhaps* pewter. *Maybe* this teapot is pewter."

Havana looks at the pot, picks it up and pours tea in her cup. She puts the pot down, taps it with her finger, gazes at it for a moment. She lifts her face and looks me in the eye. "So you're saying the color silver is in a silver teapot?"

The second biscuit wiped out, I brush a few crumbs off my T-shirt. "Good. Now, say you're looking at the Golden Gate Bridge. No, scratch that. Say you're looking up at a cloud at sunset. A beautiful purple cloud. Is the color purple in the cloud? Or you got a juicy red apple in your hand. Is the red in the apple?"

She nods her head. "This is getting deep."

I eyeball her untouched biscuit and gulp down half my espresso. "You like going deep, you've told me so. This new guy you've been seeing, Troy—you like him 'cause he's smart, math grad from Berkeley and all. He's deep. You've told me you like to go over to his place and just sit around with him and talk all night instead of heading out to the nightclubs. So, is the color purple in the cloud, is the red in the apple?"

She takes a small bite out of the biscuit. "I guess so."

"Maybe yes, maybe no, huh? What about a green apple or an orange sky?"

She mulls it over, takes it seriously. This is what intrigues me about Havana. She was the ultimate party girl in high school. She does not regret the days and nights driving around in cars, running through boys, dancing to the music and flashing her fake ID. Yet she knows she missed something along the way. She wants to be smart, but jumping over the thick line separating the educated from the rest is not easy.

"I give up," she sighs. "Tell me where the colors are."

I shrug. "Beats me. For sure the colors can't be in things or the air, apples and clouds of many hues clear that up. Are colors just in our minds or out there? I'd go with out there somewhere. Are there real colors and apparent colors? If so, how do you tell the difference? Is it all about light? Out on the farm, are all cows black at night? Maybe, but lots of brown cows when the sun comes up. Oooh, the poet's sunlight painting the world. Is that where colors come from? Not easy, colors. Like many other questions churning around out there, the answers remain elusive, or undiscovered, or maybe there are no answers. And so: maybe, sometimes, perhaps, on the other hand. At the same time, some things are certain, absolute, or true. When somebody says 'that may be true for you, but not for me,' all you're left with is a contradiction."

Havana smiles wickedly, bats her eyes. "I know something that's true silver and shouldn't be."

"Fantastic. What would that be? You going to eat the rest of that?" I ask, pointing to her plate.

She pushes it toward me, points at my forehead. "Your hair is growing out. Like brown on top and silver roots, and the brown is starting to fade. *That's* a contradiction. I'll dye it again for you."

I run my hand through my hair. "Uh, well, you said it takes twenty-four shampoos to get it out, and I figure I'm about halfway there. I'm thinking of going natural again."

"It looks great ash brown. If you let me do it again, maybe I'll cut my hair like Bianca's, just so long as I never have to see her again."

"Maybe?"

Havana gives me a cold stare. "No promises. Girl cuts her hair, that's a very big deal. Not the kind of thing I can just do on the spur of the moment. Besides, short hair on a girl seems more like a dyke thing. 'Course, I wouldn't mind if some of those asshole guys thought I was a dyke. Then they wouldn't bug me."

I go with that. "Okay, brown dye again with no preconditions. Do think you'd look really cute with short hair, though. How'd Fred like your wig last night?"

She bounces the teabag in the pot aggressively, pulls it out and sets it on the few crumbs I missed on her plate. "Now that's really stupid. First of all, it's not a wig. It's a hairpiece. A wig covers all your head. He didn't even notice. Guys can't tell a hairpiece from the real thing." She looks out the window at a cute boy passing by, turns back. "Fred seemed so . . . normal, not weirded out at all, 'cept for . . ."

"I'm not surprised. Golden showers, cock-a-doodle-do. I ran across the rooster man in this book on masochists. Amazing stuff, this one nutcake takes a live chicken with him to a whorehouse. He strangles the chicken before the hooker's eyes, then gets it on with her. He's gotta do that, or he can't get off."

"Christ, I don't want to hear this."

"Yeah, right, sorry, slipped my mind. Then there's another case kinda like Fred: guy's into cross-dressing, likes to raise his skirt and flog himself with a ruler, mainly gets off by rubbing his dick on a girl's feet, dusty feet being the best. He's not into golden showers, but when he goes to church, he feels guilty 'cause he thinks Jesus is pissing down on him from the cross. Not sure if that gets him off, but trippy. Far as the rooster man goes, guess that feather up his butt is like a stick of dynamite going off."

She reaches across the table and pokes her finger in my shoulder. "There sure was a stick of dynamite up your ass last night. You farted in my face."

"No way. I farted under the sheets."

"Why didn't you get up and go to the bathroom?"

"Can't always get ahead of that curve. Besides, it's my futon, so I have the right to pass my foul winds into the sheets."

"Maybe so, but it woulda been *polite* to get your ass up and go to the bathroom."

"Miss Manners would agree, I'm sure. Sorry about that, I know my blasts in the atmosphere could burn off the ozone layer. By the way, Hitler had chronic flatulence too. That's why he became a vegetarian. He gobbled down carrots and broccoli, figuring it would improve the odor of his farts. Didn't help, so he started eating handfuls of an anti-gas pill prescribed by his quack doctor. Stuff had strychnine in it. Didn't get him in time, though. Fucker's lower intestinal tract just kept on evacuating, cutting the cheese for Eva Braun in the bunker till the final hour."

Havana squeezes her nose. "Gross. You're a *lot* weirder than the rooster guy." She reaches out, pulls my right hand across the table, turns it palm up. "Okay, close your eyes. I'm going to give you something."

I follow in the service of my mistress. I feel wetness in my hand, open my eyes and see a soggy teabag in my palm. She leans toward me, casts off a penetrating gaze, and whispers, "Plug up your ass-hole with this."

I squeeze the teabag in my fist. "Might give it a try. Hey, maybe the E agitates the backdoor trumpet. Stuff is strong. You eat much of that chop suey?"

"Yeah, but I keep it under control. Dennis does too, but he's more into cocaine candy. Whacked out all the time. Got to the point where his face looked like it was collapsed." She presses her fingers into her cheeks, pulls down, turning her mouth into an awful crushed curl. "Freaked me out, and I thought, shit, that going to happen to me? Don't do much coke any more."

Dennis.

He is the current boyfriend with whom Havana's been living, as opposed to Troy of Berkeley, who is the latest and most promising contender for her heart. Troy burned the CD that destroyed my ears while my E-blown eyes feasted on Havana's dirty dancing. Troy plays the guitar, feeds the high-decibel results into a computer he then manipulates to make something approximating music.

By coincidence, both Havana and Shannon have recently rattled the cages of their stand-by-me's by going AWOL. Hard to say if either of them will dump their regulars for good and drown their respective guitar-slinging leaders of the band in the enormous waters of their passions. In fairness, I must point out Havana claims Shannon's identical enthusiasm is not a coincidence but a decree from a mysterious designer sprinkling the planet with synchronicity.

Shannon has an easier time playing two guys since she lives by herself, or did until her mother came to visit. Havana still lives with Dennis, sort of, using his house for a storage locker, partway satisfying his devouring need for her. As long as her discarded wigs—oops, hairpieces—continue to peek out from ever-changing piles of clothes and the scent of a dozen drained perfume bottles fills the fetid air of his unvacuumed house, Dennis can maintain the illusion they are still a couple. He's not completely off the mark. Havana will return to her beloved after a spell of couch surfing and stay for a week or two until the cycle of mutual madness begins again, and he strangles her.

Twice so far. Both times she left, saying she would never return.

After each assault, thirty calls from Dennis to her cell phone followed in a 24/7. She answered, they yelled at each other, she told him she would no longer answer his calls, but she did. He sobbed and whimpered and said never again. She returned. He crumpled into a ball at her feet, tears gushing in his eyes, said he was fat and going bald, and she was beautiful and he wasn't good enough for her. (*"Yes,"* said her Zen counselor. "That's the one thing he got right.")

Back together, Saturday rolled around, she wanted to party, and

Dennis loves strutting into the End Up, watching the heads turn with Havana on his arm. Packed, no place to sit, better, really, crushed together. A friend of theirs arrived, asked Havana to dance. She did, didn't want to stop, danced with several strangers, including a lemur-eyed catamite with a slender, perfectly proportioned bod, the ideal candidate to fulfill her greatest dream, a Stonewall of her own. "If they only knew how much I love to give head, I know I'm as good as a gay guy—hey, I'm better."

Her long legs shining under a cargo miniskirt sashayed across the End Up's dance floor back to Dennis. She's all smiles and totally up on life. He looked like a wounded Teddy bear. "This place sucks. I want to be with cool people. Let's go home."

Not wanting to upset him, she put her arms around him, a quiet embrace in the midst of music, beer, and sweat. A silent ride in Dennis's new car for a while, then he got on her case about leaving him alone at the bar, twiddling his thumbs. This astounded her. "I mean, I just like to dance. It's no big deal. *Everybody's* having a good time, except Dennis." (The counselor: "Wanting to be with cool people is a sure sign you are not cool. Now, on the dancing, I don't want to take his side, but . . . uh . . . maybe . . .")

Dennis is a thirty-one-year-old salesman, works nine to five and hates his job. Born with a silver spoon in his mouth, the spoon is usually up his nose. He shares his cocaine along with E for hors d'oeuvres with a bunch of other rich kids, drives a Lexus paid for by Mom and Dad who live in Chicago. They made the down payment on Dennis's half-million-dollar house in Pacific Heights and send him periodic checks plus or minus a few thou when Dennis calls needing an infusion of cash for his music video production venture, which remains in the planning stages.

Perfectly understandable his parents would want to help out, since he's got a full-time job and the moxie to spend nights and weekends applying his business acumen in the cultural arena. Besides that, he has the advantage of being a couple thousand miles away, so they have no idea what he's really up to.

What impressed Havana when she met Dennis was his confidence, what all women really want in a man. She moved in with him a week later. Within a few months, she realized his confidence was a façade covering up a mountain of insecurities.

How they met explains why the relationship was doomed: I introduced them. Dennis called Zen. Amazing, how many men want to win over an escort. Rarely happens. When it does, the man assures her he has no problem with her line of work; after a while he decides he must save her from a life of sin. In Havana's case, her sinning had barely begun when he met her, and hasn't improved much since. She's never around when I call her. Her rich regular, along with my number one client, Norman, who likes to see two or three girls in a long, drawn-out cocaine extravaganza, pretty much sum up her Zen resume. But Dennis thinks every moment she's not in the house with him, she's out doing a knob job on a trick.

At the outset, Dennis loved the wild girl. He still loves her, but when he gets mad: "You bitch, you're nothing but a worthless whore, get out of my house." She'll bolt when he strangles her; she'll leave when he throws her out. In both cases, she'll say it's all over, this is it, no more; then she'll return after his pleading calls.

At Café DeLucchi, Havana tells me Dennis has been on his best behavior of late. "'Cause you're not there," I say.

She nods vaguely, then throws me for a loop. "Do you think I'm stupid?"

"Stupid to move back."

"Yeah, I guess so. But that's not what I mean. Like, do you think I'm dumb?"

I do wonder if she burned off some IQ points with a long, steady diet of drugs, but I say: "Absolutely not. Some gaps in your education, but there are dumb college graduates and smart dropouts."

She's tearing up a napkin, a nervous habit of such regularity, she could be a human shredder. "Dennis graduated from college but told me he just barely made it through, only went to college 'cause his parents made him. Said if—"

"What's his degree in?" I interjected.

"Business."

"Makes sense, venture capitalist and all."

"I think *he's* stupid. Watches TV all the time. He never reads anything. Never has anything interesting to say, like"—she snaps her forefinger off her thumb against the teapot, and beams—"Whatsa color? That was really cool, how did you know all that?"

"Everything I know I steal from books. Don't you think you've tortured that napkin enough?"

She giggles and quickly drops the snowy remains on top of the dual-purpose teabag. The sun coming through the window warms her face, a face that suddenly changes, a face filled with hurt. "Last time I saw Dennis, he had some friends over. I used to like them, but now I think they're boring too. This one guy asked Dennis what's the capital of Texas or New York or someplace. Then everybody got into it, asking each other what's the capital of whatever. Three or four times Dennis asked me. Utah was one I remember, the state, I mean. I didn't know the capital."

"He gave you an easy one—Salt Lake City."

Boom. Like murder in the first degree. Tears in her eyes. First time I've seen her cry. She blots her eyes with the remaining napkin. "That's what he said, too. And in front of everybody. 'She's so fucking dumb, she doesn't know anything.' Then he starts laughing, humiliating me. And he's doing this in front of his friends, and they're laughing too."

I'm stunned. I go through a long litany trying to explain to her this is a grade school exercise, useful for memorization, but that knowing Montpelier is the capital of Vermont doesn't separate the wheat from the chaff. She nods in agreement, but I sense this wound is far from healed. "Tell me, was this worse than Dennis choking you?"

The long pause before answering is itself deadly. "Both times he did that, I thought he might kill me. But he stopped. He won't do it again, I'm sure of it."

I give her an icy gaze. "I'm not."

She turns her face away, looks out the window for a moment, then at me again, eyes still wet. "I know it was just a silly game. But it ripped me apart. Yes, it hurt more than being strangled."

FIVE

The loud grinding noise of a garbage truck picking up Dumpsters wakes me at about three in the morning. I glance out the window. A garbage man walks past a rotting sofa sitting on the curb, its innards spilling out. He shakes his head, leaves it, and heaves one last bag into a Dumpster. Seems like an appropriate time to check out my new porn DVD, *Bag Ladies.*

After I fast-forward through the credits, three whippet-thin girls appear with trash bags over their heads, painted with big eyes and big red lips. Small eyeholes cut in the bags allow the girls to see the men coming at them. The girls' red mouths warmly receive cocks slamming into larger O-shaped holes in the bags.

Okay, she's got a great bod, but you have to put a bag over her head—a stale, old message brought to you by the doofus retards in the adult film industry (and same-o in rap: "the body of a goddess and a face from hell," Warren G & Snoop Dogg).

I police porn for *Exotic* in Portland. The sex rag continues sucking up bucks in the City of Roses, even though the SF edition folded after the publisher could no longer withstand the sea of red ink. The porn DVDs I review are astonishingly boring and maddeningly similar. Adult film production companies have no reason to improve their product. *Bag Ladies* falls into the poke a hole, any hole, I'm yours category. Some men are moved by *Bag Ladies*, but far more appreciate the socially redeeming value of *Fast Times at Deep Crack High*, a popular DVD underscoring the latest turn in the sex fantasy groove: an eighteen-year-old potty-mouthed Lolita with braces on her teeth, wearing a pleated miniskirt, skipping rope in her bedroom, and pining after a fat, bald, middle-aged boomer who wears a black leather jacket and drives a Mini Cooper.

Most of the Lolita stand-ins are in their twenties. They have the shelf life of a head of lettuce. There's a new porn queen every forty-eight hours. Older women do show up in porn, but this is a niche market along with fatties, hairy ladies, bondage, spanking, golden showers, and toe sucking. Bestiality is almost nonexistent, although barnyard animals compromised by human urgencies clog the Internet. I saw one involving a woman and a horse. Lady Godiva it was not.

Above all, one genre has dominated stroke films over the past decade: anal sex. The orifice long associated with the persecution of sodomites for their unspeakable blasphemy is free at last. *Buttman Bendover Babes, When Vivid Girls Go Anal, Rocco's True Anal Stories, Sodomania,* and thousands more have celebrated every nuance of the Rear Admiral except a butt-fucking gang bang by necrophiliacs in a graveyard.

Heterosexual anal sex is following the pattern of oral sex, which burst out of the cage of unnatural acts sometime between JFK's assassination and Linda Lovelace's pillar diving in the 1972 adult tutorial *Deep Throat.* While remaining pretty much a no-no for most women, most men want to cruise the Hershey Highway. Porn resolves this tension between the sexes. The man enjoys viewing an extravaganza of doings and quiverings among lively anuses, while the woman sits out in the gazebo, reading *The Sexual Life of Catherine M.,* a situation akin to the Missouri Compromise.

They didn't call it the Show-Me State for nothing.

Enacted in 1820 as a compromise on the slavery question, Congress repealed the act in 1854, thus fueling the sectional turmoil that exploded seven years later, when the South tried to butt-fuck the North. I'm certain that within the next thirty-four years, the heterosexual anal sex dispute will be resolved, and we'll be faced with the propriety of ear and nose sex. Maybe even eyeballs. No doubt, porn will be ahead of the curve, depicting the catastrophe amidst the last remaining virgin orifices.

Humiliation and degradation of women is standard fare, frequently so far off the chart, it seems beyond misogyny. In *Snakepit,* director Gregory Dark, known for pushing the sleaze envelope into the nearest hole in hell, has a porn queen gang-banged by studs outfitted with plastic pig snouts strapped on their faces. Degrading, or infantile comedy?

In 1995, *The World's Biggest Gang Bang* featured a porn star having sex 251 times with about fifty Titanic rammers in one day. A spate of clone vids kept setting new records, including a four-hour bone-anza filmed in an airplane hangar decked out with Daytona 500 banners. The babe's back forty gets ploughed by 541 men in a grueling 12-hour jam pot penetration spectacle. This is considered female empowerment, along with girl-on-girl action that highlights the many uses of monstro dildoes and backdoor buzzers.

The collective talent of directors, cameramen, and film editors is on a par with a high school junior turning his camcorder on his friends at the prom puking beer on the gym floor. Amongst a million DVDs of mindnumbing junk, foreplay and tenderness are unknown; double penetrations abound, usually with the girl impaled while spread-eagled on a pool table. Fingerings, spankings, squirtings, toyings, butt-pluggings, and dicks diving into the gravy run nonstop. "The Money Shot," great globs of spermatozoa splattering across the girl's face, is essential. All these gynecologic close-ups of kidney-buster lobcocks and panting vaginas remind me of the classic Army 16-millimeter black-and-white syphilitic noir shown in my high school health class. (A victory for abstinence, that training film. Haul it out of the Pentagon vault for the current crop of teens and dump the condom-over-a-banana demos.) But there is hope. Lately, the "money shot" is getting shoved aside by porn's new discovery: "the internal cum shot," or fucking.

The target market for hardcore cherry splitters is men of all colors from eighteen to ninety-two. Softcore vids, mainly for women, do manage to create a mood of intimacy, best exemplified by director Candida Royalle, whose films are far better than the routine plummetings in the maligned aperture. But in the end, Royalle's vids suffer the same fate as hardcore—lame dialogue, vapid musical scoring, slo-mo camerawork drowning in clichés.

One notable exception on planet porn: many of the gay vids are erotic, tasteful, filled with languorous teasing and a sensibility that suggests the life-enhancing dimension of porn.

I make it through twenty minutes of *Bag Ladies*, scratch out a few notes for "Another Lonely Night with Flagstone Walker," my column in *Exotic* (xmag.com). Flagstone is a pen name I adopted when I started writing for *Screw*. My nom de guerre is a free pass that allows a reckless rage I ordinarily keep caged to overtake my writing.

Flagstone slips in *Rocco in London*, a DVD that opens with Rocco asking a glossy permed blonde, "Are you from Poland?" After the thong-clad cutie confirms she's a Warsaw refugee, Rocco asks if he can piss in her mouth. "I guess so," she says matter-of-factly. Thankfully, he does not. She tosses her hair back, gets down on all fours, shakes her ass, then lip dances on Rocco's rude javelin. Ten seconds later, Rocco's buried in another blonde's spunk pot; the name "Jake" is tattooed on her inner thigh a half-inch below her tight denim shorts. He turns over Jake's honey, rips off her shorts, and pumps a fresh load in her ass. Then Rocco concludes: "English girls suck a different way." They do not, a moot point since Jake's honey speaks with an Eastern European accent. Next up, a yummy Italian who says "So rude" when Rocco sticks his fingers up her vertical smile twelve seconds after meeting her. (This is the only moment in Rocco Everywhere-but-in-London that rings true.)

Flagstone takes a break, taps his speed ration out of a baggie, replaces the baggie in a leather slot in his Day Planner. He snorts the line, puts in another DVD. Nothing in *DP Penitentiary* rings true, at the Maximum Security Prison for Troubled Females, where the warden, an enlightened and caring official who seeks only to rehabilitate wayward girls, tells a first-time offender, porn star Keegan Skky, "The female species thinks with its taint."

Over the centuries, philosophers have located the mind in the head, the heart, the liver, or floating around outside the body. A porn breakthrough here, discovering women hide their most intimate thoughts in the delicate area between the glory hole and the booty hole. The warden says female prisoners' taints must be massaged "so the lesser sex can become more docile." This program is pursued with a vengeance. Keegan Skky is wearing a chain-gang striped uniform that is quickly doffed for jail therapy—a platoon of guards, along with the warden, hammering away in her duck butter.

Flagstone's about porned out, but *Crème de la Face* sits on his desk littered with empty beer cans, peanut bags, and words. He'll hang in for the lame-o French accented title. Flagstone is riveted to the opening scene with Rodney and Allison much the same way crowds in seventeenth-century Paris got off watching the ritualistic disembowelment of a prisoner after his execution. You don't really want to look, but something compels you to stick it out. In this case, it's what Rodney is saying, while Allison, on her knees, sucks him off: "Do you know how many times I'll compliment a girl and get shot down? Do you know how many times that happens?"

Rodney whines on about the abuse he has suffered from women who regard him as the weenie he is. With Rodney's sad serpent between her lips, Allison bobs her head up and down, and grunts her sympathy. Rodney yammers on: "You can make up for all those girls in the past who I wanted to have sex with, and they didn't think I was good enough for them!"

Superb porn marketing. The guy watching can identify with Rodney and dream of the day a girl like Allison comes along, which will never happen. Even if it did, it wouldn't matter. He'd blow it, and then go buy some more porn.

It's as good an excuse as any.

SIX

Flagstone Walker bounces about like a yo-yo on a string, a camcorder against his right eye, preparing to film what he's convinced will be a breakthrough in the adult biz: the first in a projected series of fifteen-minute softcore political porn epics. He's on location in his office on the fourth floor of the Grant Building, formerly the offices of *Exotic* magazine, its logo still stenciled on the smoky pebbled glass door, shielding the apparatus of Zen's criminal enterprise within.

Flagstone dips at the knees, his feverish dreams hopped up, a camcorder directly in front of his quarry. He carefully calculates the composition for the first and only scene in the ten- to fifteen-minute film, Shannon and Havana's extemporaneous dialogue on a significant political question, followed by a g/g.

Flagstone has decided he must do more than review porn. He feels compelled to throw down the gauntlet against the industry by beheading the double penetration, a move he deliriously compares to literary critics Mary McCarthy and James Wood blowing the whistle on novelists, and then bursting forth with their own engaging curios. Flagstone's project will adhere to the Tractarian principles published in a broadside under the rubric Dogma 95. The screaming red headline, metaphorically nailed to Hollywood's door by Danish filmmakers Lars von Trier and Thomas Vinterberg, demanded a return to austere, low-budget, no-frills films eschewing the formulaic story arc and the Hollywood enchanters' insistence on thrill-a-minute-soaked spectacle.

Flagstone is most impressed by the Danes' "vow of chastity" that can rescue film from its deflowering by a gregarious pack of unrestrained hacks. A Dogma 95 project seeks to snatch a morsel of truth from everyday life using the first principle of cinematic technique—a handheld camera with only available light. To ensure *vérité sans peur,* the director must strive to remove any trace of his own personality from the film, and leave his name off the credits, though Flagstone will violate this tenet and forego Dogma 95's imprimatur on the grounds "truth without fear" will be better served with his name boldly stamped on a black frame in foot-high white sans serif type.

The girls sit next to each other, Shannon in an old wooden swivel chair and Havana in a tall, adjustable steel frame task chair (both scooped up by Flagstone from across the hall when Promise, a nonprofit that generously doled out counseling, condoms, tampons, Slurpees, and giant Hawaiian pizzas to the city's street harlots, moved out of the Grant to an office in the Tenderloin, a sensible administrative decision insuring closer access to Promise's community of soiled doves). Flagstone appreciates the abandoned furniture, but regrets the fourth-floor hallway no longer echoes with the musical stampede of skyscraper high heels from the bottom of the trade, a few steps and a thousand miles away from the Zen dolls.

Trying to find the best shooting angle, Flagstone's long legs advance around the chairs in an exaggerated stride he believes to be smooth as Fred Astaire. He backs up a few feet, bumps into the table, and knocks over a stack of CDs including Keith Jarrett, Keiko Matsui, Miles, Dylan, Randy Newman, Cowboy Junkies, and *The Fine Lookin' Hits of Eddie Cochran.*

Havana points to a Britney Spears CD on the floor. "You like her?"

"Uh, strictly for professional reasons," he says, picking up the CDs. "I'm writing a story on Brit. The tabloids keep pounding on her for losing her virginity, and parents are up in arms 'cause she's a bad influence on their thirteen-year-old daughters wearing thongs that peek out over the tops of their jeans. Thing is, Britney's spent her teen years waving the Bible and preaching save-it-till-you're-married. So even if that asshole Justin Timberlake finally banged her, she held off till she was almost twenty-one. What more could a parent ask? I bet she's still very religious and quite conservative, despite her always-exposed midriff. She's the good girl pretending to be bad, the pop queen sending out America's traditional cultural message—the mixed signal."

Havana frowns. "A hypocrite."

Shannon pipes up. "Are you taping this? Like a movie about two girls talking about Britney!"

"No, Britney won't work for this."

"Britney's over," Havana asserts, disappointing Flagstone, since he just pointed out the cultural import of Britney's virginity, the central theme of his 1,500-word jewel currently glimmering in *The New Republic* slushpile.

High bookshelves, two desks (a small refrigerator and toaster oven on one, a computer on the other), filing cabinets and stacks of cardboard boxes filled with more files are buttressed against three walls in Flagstone's small office. Too much background clutter for a clean shot. Flagstone pulls a large quilt out of the closet. "Let's get rid of the chairs." As the girls push them against the door, the quilt's kaleidoscope of colors sprinkle across the sunlit floor. Shannon's luminous blue eyes open wide. "That's so-o-o-o beautiful. Where did you get it?"

"My grandmother made it. She'd sit in her rocking chair for hours on end, make quilts and read *Science and Health*. That's a book Christian Scientists read along with the Bible."

Shannon drops down on all fours, rolls over on the quilt, shoots her Catholic schoolgirl kneesocked legs in the air. A patch of white cotton panties pops into view under her short pleated skirt, the nymphet subtext for Flagstone's vow of chastity on film. "Well, I'd say your grandma's religion was way cool," she says, as her arms stretch out and slide across the quilt.

Havana, wearing a light blue thong and a white croptop, steps behind the tall office chair, grips the back of it. "Religion sucks," she insists. "It's stupid to believe in God." She leans into the chair, rapidly kicking her right leg back, toning her already firm butt, prompting a "go, girl" from Shannon, who sits up on the quilt and lights a Kool.

"You need to eliminate the word 'stupid' from your vocabulary. Would you say Cecil Williams feeding all those homeless people at Glide Memorial is stupid?"

"No, I didn't mean that, and I'll try not saying stupid, but you say it, so why shouldn't I?"

"The word never slips off my tongue," says Flagstone. Watching her switch legs around rep twenty, he raises his hand and slowly traces the outline of her butt before her eyes. "If it ever falls, it will be the end of Western Civilization."

"Don't worry, not a chance. You called Dennis a 'stupid fuck.'" Flagstone pours a bag of speed on the desk, inspects the white-encrusted tooter and snorts a match-thin half-inch line, a ludicrous ritual of rationing he always undermines by follow-ups that will ultimately burn a hole in his nose.

Shannon sucks the smoke deep into her lungs, exhales and piles on. "Stupid to snort speed."

"That's right," Havana seconds.

Flagstone ignores the drug counseling from Shannon the pot smoker and Havana of E. "Dennis is a stupid fuck, but not the people who believe in God, most of them, at any rate. Religion provides a great deal of comfort to the multitudes. The first mover never moved me, but the Holy Spirit lives in that quilt."

"Amen," shouts Shannon. She leans over and kisses the quilt.

Havana's nut-brown legs slide away from Promise's chair/exercise machine, move in front of the long mirror installed on the closet door by a non-negotiable demand from the courtesans. She pulls a few strands of hair out of Flagstone's brush, not nearly enough to suit him. He says nothing, makes a mental note to get another, probably the fifth or sixth brush under her lost luggage wave, not to mention cigarette lighters that disappear within twenty-four hours after purchase. Shannon's equally guilty of this misdemeanor.

The Daughter of Cuba strides jauntily over to the desk, draws a Camel Light Wide out of Flagstone's pack, and asks: "So, are we going to make a movie?"

Flagstone's lanky frame bends to the side as he makes a grand gesture with his arm, indicating Havana sit on the quilt. She does. "Okay if we smoke?"

"Yes, both of you, and the more gratuitous the better. All those ninnies in the fascist nonsmoking brigade drive me nuts."

"Fascist? What's that mean?" Havana queries.

"Like Hitler," Flagstone answers, but quickly backs off the analogy while simultaneously thinking his cinematic project might exceed his expectations with a strike on the mother lode. "No, that's unfair. The nonsmoking fanatics are not like Hitler. Intolerant, for sure, but they just want to snuff out all cigarettes, not snuff us out in the gas chamber."

Flagstone once again begins loping around the girls, awkwardly attempting to imitate the moves of the fashion photographer in Antonioni's *Blow Up*, a classic film he'd rented the previous night for inspiration. The girls giggle, watching the camcorder bob and weave over their heads.

Flagstone suddenly realizes shooting down on them is an insidious method of visual authoritarianism, a gross violation of the Dogma 95 code. He drops down on both knees. Good, very good, the bookcase behind them blurry enough to prevent vertical lines from cutting into their heads, the hazy sunlight coming through the huge office window casting a soft glow over Shannon's lush milky skin and Havana's lusty olive complexion—just what he'd envisioned, two goddesses in thong and pleated skirt posing in a silent *tableau vivant*.

Problem, though. Cameraman has the shakes. A jittering duo in the viewfinder.

Unaware that the burning excitement in his squinting eye serves only to illuminate the barren wilderness of his speed-fed mind, Flagstone attributes his twitchings to a pusher at Peet's Coffee in the financial district who slides the bills through his collection-practiced fingers with such grace, it comes off like a tender gesture, making Flagstone feel the coffee is free. Even at six in the morning, during the *faux*-essayist's thirty-fourth hour on the buzz, the pusher's large round face flashes a smile, a huge clown's smile that always kindly overlooks his regular tweaked customer's occasional rude transgression. Flagstone imports into Peet's a semisweet chocolate chip cookie purchased at Specialty's bakery a block away, the contraband discreetly tucked away in the fold of the *Chronicle*, possibly a properly edited "Insight" section.

"What do you want us to do besides smoke?" asks Shannon, squashing her Kool in the ashtray, and immediately lighting another. Havana looks purposely at her own cigarette fuming above her polished pink nails. "Should we talk about smoking fascists, or wait, nonsmoking fascists, right?"

"Right. I want the dialogue between both of you to flow naturally, so it could spin off on the nonsmoking Hitler sidebar, but the question that sets the film in motion should remain central," says Flagstone, as he sends another line up his right nostril, figuring once wrecked, twice won't matter. He then screws the camcorder on the tripod, figuring with equal unreason that it's not totally dishonorable to bust Dogma 95's hand-held camera rule on the grounds that vice is juicing his jitters. The author of his own punishment, he assures himself, should at least be given a chance to prevail as a steady auteur.

Havana pulls her sweet knees up to her chest. "So the film begins with you asking us a question about politics. Maybe you should let us in on the question so we can prepare a little."

Flagstone, on his knees in front of the tripod, frowns. "The question is so profound, it is the title of this film. Knowing the question in advance would destroy the work of art."

With animal brightness in her eyes, Shannon sends a hard gaze toward Flagstone, stretches out her right leg, slowly pulls up her pleated skirt. "Art?"

Havana follows suit with the sound of one thong snapping.

"Drop those moves in at any moment when they advance the storyline," says Flagstone, blowing his nose on a Kleenex.

A forefinger rises in the air, a loud voice off camera. *"Who is Thomas Jefferson?"*

Puzzled expressions sweep across our costars' faces. Havana blinks. Shannon tilts her head about an inch to one side, then freezes up, her cigarette perfectly positioned in her upraised hand. Havana's cigarette hangs off her lip, quite uncharacteristic for her, perhaps an affectation for the film, but it registers like a cannon firing across the silent sea. Three seconds of silence; three seconds with barely a move by either of them. Flagstone had a hunch the question might stump them, but the long pause still jolts him. Holy shit, this is better than Clint Eastwood's "Go ahead, make my day," he thinks, pure and simple silence hiding nothing, the blank slate as an epiphany.

Flagstone thought he might break into laughter if this happened; instead, he finds himself struggling along with them in their search for the answer. It may yet bubble up, for he knows Jefferson has valiantly waved and continues to wave the Declaration of Independence in front of the onrushing tide of all students, including juvenile delinquents.

A tentative, frustrated "Damn, I know who Thomas Jefferson is" from Shannon breaks the silence, but the impression on her memory remains weak, slips out stillborn, as she says, "Right on the tip of my tongue." Sitting cross-legged on the quilt, she reveals the innocence of Lolita the director seeks without directing. She turns her head toward Havana. "I think he might be a movie star . . . " She trails off, asks Flagstone, "You said Thomas Jefferson. Is it usually Tom Jefferson?"

"Like Tom Hanks," Havana adds helpfully. Both laugh.

"Thomas Jefferson," Flagstone says. Havana extinguishes her cigarette, rolls from her sitting position, stretches out on her stomach, arches her back, elbows on the quilt, chin cupped in her hands. The director slowly zooms back to capture the stream of sunlight on meaningful curves.

Shannon continues plowing contemporary celebrity ground. "I recognize that name from movies . . . " This train of perceptions gets her nowhere until her Kool stabs the air with "not an actor, there was a movie *about* Thomas Jefferson."

Flagstone's head rapidly jerks up and down, suggesting this engine should be stoked. He recalls the film *Jefferson in Paris*, starring Nick Nolte, but says nothing.

Havana pushes herself up, sits down and crosses her legs, making for a matched set. "Politics, though, has to be about someone in politics. Can I try one of these?" she says, picking up Shannon's pack of Kools. "Sure" comes the reply. Havana lights up, takes a tiny drag, poofs out the menthol with a smoking fetish O. "I remember something about that movie, a poster maybe. Didn't see it, I'm sure. Seems like it was a love story. Thomas Jefferson and a woman in his arms and . . . costumes." She closes her eyes, costumes swirl in the mind's closet until the door swings open wide. "Thomas Jefferson's dead! Like, he's a famous person in history."

Flagstone feels like he's finally been released from Torquemada's rack, his crushed bones healing in freedom's sunshine. Both girls excitedly nod their heads at slightly different rates. Shannon rolls out the history dice. "Was Thomas Jefferson the president who got killed? The one who . . . didn't he fuck Marilyn Monroe?"

Under the baleful gaze of huge snake eyes, Havana dissents. "No, that was John Kennedy."

Shannon cringes. "Right, I shoulda known that."

Fact checker's voice off camera: "More likely Bobby Kennedy, the president's brother, did Marilyn. Maybe John too, still a lotta argument on that zipper. Or zippers. John Kennedy was assassinated. People are killed, presidents are assassinated."

Shannon's got the dice again. "Yeah, and Kennedy wasn't the only one assassinated. But I don't think Thomas . . . Jefferson . . . it was . . . " She looks to Havana for help.

None there. Flagstone decides a critical interruption does not violate Dogma 95's regulations. "You probably have Abraham Lincoln in mind."

A big smile over a perfect set of white teeth on a trade from a Vegas dentist and a blast of blue off Shannon's eyes. "Yeah, that's it. He freed the slaves!"

"Right, during the Civil War," says Flagstone, inadvertently opening up the sidebar for Havana, who rapidly infers the motion of one billiard ball on the table will smash into another. "The Civil War? So that was to stop Hitler?"

Flagging Flagstone: "No, two separate things. Hitler was the bad guy, the ultimate evil fuck on the planet during World War II. We went to war against Hitler after Pearl Harbor on December 7, 1941, a big date in history."

"I saw *Pearl Harbor*," says Shannon. "It was great."

Havana disagrees. "It was okay, kinda yucky romantic, though."

Flagstone surveys the billiard ball at rest. "The Civil War was about a hundred years earlier, 1861 to 1865. North. South. Lincoln assassinated" (a nod to Shannon). "*Gone With the Wind.* Now, who is Thomas Jefferson?"

"Forgot about him," Shannon teases.

Havana sets her half-burnt Kool on the ashtray, stares down intently at her curled right hand, and begins pushing on the cuticle of her little finger with her left thumb. Possibly a genuine Dogma 95 moment, despite Flagstone mouthing a painful silent "no" while his open palms desperately fan left and right. His preemptive strike on the whole damn manicure fails; Havana continues her diggings, but Shannon sees the camcord artist's open wound, slaps her sister's thigh, and says, "Hey, who T.J.?"

Havana quickly smiles and snaps her thong in repentance. "Let's see—" She touches her lower lip thoughtfully with her forefinger— "Thomas . . . Jefferson . . . Thomas . . . Thomas . . . I know that name. . . . "

Shannon nods her head toward Havana, encouraging her to go deep. Havana thrusts her hand in the air. "I know! Thomas Jefferson was the guy that invented the light bulb."

Flagstone coolly responds, "Half-right. That was Thomas

Edison," thinking, oh man, the *Dirty Harry* line is nothing compared to this!

"Thomas Edison, right," says Havana. "Now I remember. Read something about his inventions in school. I remember something in school about Thomas Jefferson too, but I give up."

Shannon sticks up her thumb. "Me too."

Flagstone persists: "Don't give up yet. Here's a hint. The Declaration of Independence."

Shannon beams. "Like Fourth of July, the thing they read before the fireworks."

"Thomas Jefferson wrote that thing," says Flagstone. He shuts off the camcorder, tries as best he can in two minutes to fill them in on the American Revolution, grabs a book and flips to the appendix. He reads them the opening paragraphs on life, liberty, and the pursuit of happiness, then jumps to the last line: "And for the support of this Declaration, with firm reliance on the Protection of Divine Providence, we mutually pledge to each other our Lives, our Fortunes, and our Sacred Honor."

Havana strokes her arm. "That gives me chills. It's so powerful, so beautiful."

Somehow, so is she.

SEVEN

All afternoon and into the night, the cast and crew of *Who is Thomas Jefferson?* snort speed, drop E, smoke pot and polish off two bottles of Merlot. They feast on a smorgasbord of pink ham, slices of turkey breast, dry salami, Havarti cheese, Carr's crackers, grapes, and strawberries piled high on paper plates.

Havana and Shannon have viewed the cassette on the camcorder's LCD monitor about thirty times, going gaga over their low-wattage historical brain power. "Hey, why don't you have us try to name state capitals?" giggles Havana.

Flagstone is pleased she's lightening up on Dennis's mean-spirited quiz. "Won't fit with T.J., but maybe for another vid," he suggests, placing the camcorder to his eye. "Let's ease into the g/g. Dance around a while and then get down."

Troy's infernal CD blasts out of the speakers, the office aglow with candlelight and a strong beam from a tensor lamp on the desk. Long brown hair whips across Havana's face as she shakes and grinds her hips with her back turned before Shannon, who leans against the wall in a sultry pinup pose. Havana turns 180 degrees on her toes, exposing the back of her thong running up the crease of her butt. Shannon pushes away from the wall, throws her head back, struts toward Havana, just as a blood-curdling scream from the street rises above the sound of an equally horrific guitar riff.

Flagstone swings over to the window, eye glued to the viewfinder, a *tirailleur* drawing the fury of fire in the street. Possibly weave in documentary footage of the street dwellers with the g/g, he muses as the girls rush to the window next to him. Havana throws it open, leans out over the ledge. The screamer is a tall white woman in a baggy coat. She's standing in the middle of the street in front of a Toyota, cursing the driver. "You fuckin' tryin' to run me down?"

She bangs her fist on the Toyota's hood. The driver remains behind the wheel, doesn't honk the horn. The woman stands there for a while, finally steps to one side, looks left and right like a tiger about to strike. The Toyota slowly moves forward, a man appears behind it, rushes the woman and grabs her from behind. She struggles free, turns, slaps him on the face. He slaps her harder with an open hand. "Leave her alone," screams Havana.

The guy looks up at the silhouette framed in the fourth-floor window, a vision in a thong and tanktop cut an eighth of an inch below her breasts. "Sure will if you come down," he yells. Havana flips him off. He laughs, the woman waves to Havana, then the couple embrace with a deep kiss.

"That's better," Havana yells, overjoyed at having quelled a domestic dispute.

The lovebirds walk arm in arm back to the sidewalk in front of the Court of Appeals. In the daytime, little foot traffic moves in and out of the palatial fortress other than an occasional black-robed judge, who steps out of a limo and swooshes silently into the chambers of high justice for the Far West.

In the hours of darkness, gargoyles perched on the ledge of the Court of Appeals look directly across Seventh into a vast pit surrounded by a chain-link fence that has been ripped out in several spots. The openings provide easy access for the junkies who scurry into a pop-and-slam den underneath the remaining pillars of the Greyhound Bus Lines terminal, gutted years ago.

After the junkie drives a needle into a vein that has not yet collapsed, he crawls out of the pit, back into the street where the War on Drugs has stalled into a permanent standoff between the cops and dealers, the war at its peak on this night, as it always is on the last day of the month. The homeless are queuing up for their SSI checks, cash grants from the city, or any other stipend offered through various human service agencies sewing patches in the social safety net. The checks are sent directly to a cash cow on the corner of Seventh and Market, the Money Mart check cashing outlet, that skims about seven percent off the top. The line forms under a bright yellow neon sign: PAYDAY LOANS   CHECKS CASHED   24 HRS. The parade starts at the stroke of midnight, when the checks are released.

The novel feature of the current system is a wonder to behold. In effect, city, state, and federal agencies license crack, coke, smack, and speed to the homeless, about half of whom are mentally ill. To be sure, this does require a middleman absolving the government of any responsibility. The recipients pick up their checks, exit from the Money Mart into a sea of China White. The drug retailers hanging around offer a full-service package to those who are spun out or nuts, or spun out *and* nuts. The dealers operate with discretion in nearby alleys or boldly sell their product across the street in Civic Center Plaza in front of the Carl Jr.'s.

Are all of the homeless tweaking? No. Some who use their checks for food and rent rest on the sidewalk next to the rock smokers. Among those with all their worldly goods in shopping carts are men who want jobs, battered women tossed out of their homes, and children for whom the American Dream has already been erased.

Shannon points to a couple of guys huddled in the doorway of the Odd Fellows Hall across the street, passing a burning crack pipe between their hands. "Get them in the movie."

Flagstone does, then pans the jumpy camcorder up the five-story ornate façade of the building, zooms in on the huge engraved panel of the All-Seeing Eye above a crescent moon surrounded by stars, the eye's omnipresence neglecting to save the souls below from oblivion. Flagstone giggles over his easy capture of the Orwellian eye in his work in progress, compared to his hesitation long ago when confronted with the big eye of God over the door of a Cao Dai pagoda.

He stops filming, steps back for an interior shot of two lovely rear ends leaning out the window, convinced the cut from the sacred big eye to the bun quatrain is an imminent Dogma 95 visual quip.

A shot of three hard-boiled eggs sitting on his desk next to a banana.

A shot of a wide brown belt inlaid with red diamond-shaped chunks of leather snaked around a pair of black boots, left in his office by Cheyenne, Zen dolls' spirited femme lesbian, who once said, "I can't believe the number of guys who will pay to eat pussy, this makes no sense."

A shot of the bookshelf lined with paperbacks about Hitler, raw material for Flagstone's obsession in progress, a pile of words he believes is a path-breaking work on the psychotic dictator's sex life entitled *Hitler the Toilet.* This includes a scurrilous report on Hitler's golden shower. On a spring afternoon in 1930, Hitler wore his favorite uniform when Geli Raubal came for a visit: black trousers and a khaki military lounge jacket without insignia. Geli dished him up his favorite meal, a porridge soup made of flour, butter, and caraway seeds. When finished with his soup, Hitler gazed longingly at Geli, a pretty, not barely legal seventeen-year-old, his half-niece. (Geli's mother was Hitler's half-sister.) According to Otto Strasser, an early confidant of Hitler who fled to Canada after his brother Gregor was murdered by an opposing faction of Nazis, Hitler liked Geli to "squat over his face where he could examine her at close range, and this made him very excited. When the excitement reached its peak, he demanded that she urinate on him." Flagstone believes this secondhand testimony given to the OSS during the war, but he does note in his manuscript that many historians consider Strasser to be an unreliable source.

A shot of cigarette butts in an ashtray.

A shot of a painting on the wall by Richard May, an abstract expressionist work consisting of four horizontal series of white blocks outlined in black on a yellow field, each series of blocks growing into larger vertical forms resting on black lines running across the painting. The doors of perception, Flagstone suggested to Richard, who was deeply offended by his barbaric aesthetic reductionism.

Flagstone rapidly pans the camera away from the painting, zeroes in on his office door for a couple of seconds to piss off Richard, stops the camcorder. He sets it up again on the tripod mount in front of the open window and takes in the panorama below: the sidewalk aswarm with bony-limbed winos scratching their crotches, boosters taking orders for Gap and Diesel clothes, dime-baggers pulling balloons of crack out of their mouths, zoomers selling talcum powder as the devil's dandruff.

A shot lingers for a moment on a cop car spraying a searchlight across the sea of the hammered. The beam of light slides over the line of people stretched out from the entrance of the Money Mart on down the block past 7th Street Haircutters, Ming Kee Thrift store, Economy Fine Food, and Travelers Liquors where all three cash registers ring with boisterous cries pursuing the inalienable rights to a forty-ouncer.

One cop gets out of the car, saunters over toward a man curled up in a ball under a brown blanket, lightly pokes around him with his boot. A scraggly head appears above the blanket, a brief conversation follows, and the cop moves on. He walks into a big blast of white on the dark street, a new nightclub with a freshly painted white metal gate in front of a white façade and a white doorway. On the corner by the alley, the nightclub occupies the first floor of a smaller building next to the Odd Fellows Hall.

A shot of a bouncer standing in front of the white door warily eyeing the street people. End of improvised docu segment.

Flagstone pulls a plastic bird's nest out of a box, proudly displays it before the girls. "Where'd you get that?" asks Shannon.

"A toy store. I want both of you to lie in wait under the quilt. I'll film your faces looking into the bird's nest. Pretend to be witches. Wave—"

"I *am* a witch," Havana announces.

"That's even better, real and all. Wave your fingers over the nest and mumble like witches cooking something up, say 'bubble, bubble, toil and trouble,' things like that."

Havana balks. "We should do this later, get some witch costumes. I can do some Santeria."

"That would be great. Let's do this first for a trial run," says Flagstone, setting the bird's nest on the carpet. (He's still so spun out, he fails to realize he's dragging this supposed g/g scene deep into boring territory.)

"Yeah, I feel kinda witchy tonight," says Shannon. She grabs the quilt, drapes it over herself, thrusts open one side so Havana can enter the lair. They laugh and hip hug, then fall in front of the bird's nest, mumble and hum as their stormy fingers hover over the prey. Flagstone films this for about fifteen seconds, then while zooming slowly in on the bird's nest, intones a deep voiceover: "The witches' hot hearts burn with the death quivers of men. In this bird's nest high above the colony of blight, the witches have placed a dozen hewed-off penises once quenched in the fires of lust. Now they wiggle about like living members. Is there any escape for them? *Shazam!*"

Flagstone smashcuts back to Richard May's painting. He considers adding to the voiceover, "Perhaps they can escape through the doors of perception," but decides against this, figuring his refined audience for Dogma 95 political porn will easily grasp the meaning conveyed in a higher degree through the animated spirit of visual verisimilitude.

"It's a wrap," says Flagstone, rewinding the cassette.

Havana swirls her fingers around the inside of the bird's nest, turns it over, and shakes it. "No wiggling penises here."

Flagstone jumps back. "Look out! They've escaped. My God, here come ten of them." The fingers on his shaking hand scurry around her thong. She slaps his hands. "I'm going to do some Santeria on you."

By the window, Shannon's restless eyes survey the goings-on below. "We should check out that new club."

Flagstone and Havana look over her shoulder. Fashion victims standing around in seen-everything, done-it-all stances are waiting to get in the club—including, Flagstone notices with a bemused smile, a lanky girl wearing pegged pants, her hair pulled back in a ponytail, the return of Long Tall Sally. A handsome man in a dark suit and three girls pour out of a taxi. The bouncer drops the velvet rope, waves his arm, clears a path through the crowd for the designated cool. "How they rate?" asks Shannon.

"Guy owns the club, or he's a major cocaine dealer, or he's a movie producer, or he owns a few skyscrapers—whatever it is, he's a player," Flagstone replies, thinking the guy sure looks like Supervisor Gavin Newsom.

"You're a player," croaks Shannon.

"Let's go down and check it out," Havana suggests.

She slips her shrink-wrapped pants on over her thong. The trio heads outside and joins the crowd. Flagstone tells the girls to stay put, approaches the bouncer, tells him he freelances for the *Chronicle* and there's a story in a new club rejuvenating the blighted street. "Got a press pass?" asks the bouncer.

Flagstone looks him straight in the eye. "If anybody ever flashes you a press pass to get in, it's probably fake. I got a bunch of stories in my office across the street in the Grant. I can go back and get you some if you want."

"Damn, I think you're telling the truth."

Flagstone nods. "What's the name of this place?"

"Doesn't have a name yet, I'd like to name it White."

"How about White Line?"

He frowns. "Hmmm, like it, but I don't think the owner would go for it. He's thinking maybe Cloud 9. Like that?"

"Like White better, but Cloud 9's nice too. Uh, can I bring my friends?" Flagstone points toward the girls. "We won't stay too long."

The bouncer checks out the Zen duo, leers. "Definitely."

Flagstone waves them over, wishing only they would glide elegantly toward the white door instead of rushing it like Reds storming the Winter Palace.

Once inside, both excitedly ask how he did it. Later Flagstone tells them, but for the moment he puffs himself up and says: "I'm a player." Not a player for "Insight," though. Flagstone will write the story, but ultimately it bounces back on his e-mail, followed by a further blow to his ego when he picks up the Sunday paper and sees *two* pieces dripping with drama on the plight of the homeless.

Nice decor: white walls, white semicircular booths, white statues, white bar, and white staircase leading up to a small white second level where the other player stands in front of his three girls scrunched together on a white divan. Flagstone gets a closer look. Not Gavin Newsom.

The trio goes back downstairs. Havana sizes up the crowd, many dressed in sharp black clothes, neatly groomed, mostly in their thirties. "Yuppie B & T."

Flagstone slaps her arm. "Hey, don't be so hard on the East Bay. They got a right to party here."

She snorts, looks over at the deejay standing behind a small turntable cutting electronica grooves. Loud but mellow. Havana's unmoved, Shannon uninterested.

"Well, we've seen it. Shall we go?" Flagstone asks. Both girls concur. Outside, Flagstone thanks the bouncer. Walking back to the Grant, he hears his cell ring. *"Norman,* great to hear from you." All three break into a run.

With Zen's number one client on the cell, Rimbaud's line, "I is somebody else," jolts me into action. I speed-dial Cheyenne, hope she's not preoccupied with her latest, a butch dyke fire engine driver.

She can make it. I breathe a sigh of relief. Bounding up the stairs to the office in front of the girls, I shout, "He wants *four.*" Another call to Mariko, another break. She too can flash.

EIGHT

What Norman does for a living remains a mystery, but he has enough money for occasional marathons with Zen dolls at his condo in South Beach, a newly fabricated upscale neighborhood at the bottom of Embarcadero. Perhaps he's one of the many libertarian dot-commers who made a quick pile on dubious start-up operations. They do live the good life in this new precinct of wealth, flying first class to Rio, filling their condos and lofts with classic Italian furniture, scarfing down the *prix fixe* at French restaurants, leasing Lexuses, and tossing green at my girls. All booms bust, so Zen is doing its best to get the money before South Beach is invaded with process servers.

Norman likes to kick off around three in the morning with one girl for a few hours, proceed through the day and into the evening, the Zen train hurtling past his door, dropping off passengers for his entertainment. He's a New York City native, talks nonstop, mainly uninspired rants about San Francisco being a provincial city.

Norman hates everything about the city, including the best restaurants, none of which can compare to those in the Big Apple. Why he lives in a city he despises, I don't know. San Francisco is the woman you fall in love with the moment you see her. Doesn't matter whether you've lived here ten years or ten minutes, it's your city the first time you feel the high winds off the Golden Gate.

Norman insists the escort arrive right on time, a perfectly reasonable demand, given the price. This is a continual sore spot for me, with respect to other clients as well, since tardiness seems to be in the genes of all escorts. Norman also insists the girl arrive by cab. He has a paranoid streak, convinced that if I drive them, the private security guards cruising the streets around his complex will somehow know the gold pile is a floating bordello. The guards will then radio for police backup, storm his condo, and haul him off to jail. I'm sure his main concern is getting nailed for the mountain of coke piled on his Art Deco glass table.

Havana takes the first shift, returns in time for breakfast with a thousand dollars in her purse, the usual price break for three hours stretching to four, quite acceptable, given Norman's largess. This includes French wine (since all California wine is swill), takeout from a nearby deli with acceptable soft cheese and goose patés (though not up to Manhattan standards), and cocaine, a moot point in the SF/NYC competition due to its origin in Colombia or Peru or Bolivia or Venezuela, or wherever the coca crop has been pushed to escape eradication under the American government's permanently failed policy of aerial fumigation.

Over breakfast at the XYZ in the teched-out chrome and mirrored glass ambiance of the W Hotel, where Havana is partial to mimosas, I chow down on wheat pancakes. Havana sips her drink, sets it down next to her cappuccino heavily dusted with chocolate, talks about Norman. "Last time I saw him we had sex. This time he was so coked out, he didn't even ask."

I shrug. "That's what usually happens. He doesn't seem to care if he can't get it up, just as long as a girl's there to listen to him."

Havana keeps looking at the clock, waiting for 9 A.M. to strike so she can blow some dough at Nordstrom as soon as the doors open. Sensing her need, I push the pancakes aside and wave to the waitress for the check. Havana grandly hands her a hundred-dollar bill. When she returns with the change, Havana fans through the bills and hands her a ten. After receiving a warm thank-you from the waitress, Havana replies, "My horoscope said money would come my way, and it did. I want to keep the luck running."

"Great," the waitress replies, "I'm sure the stars are on a roll."

We split, and I drop her off two minutes before the shopping spree bell. I return to my office, intending to crank out some copy for the *Chronicle*, but first a quick nap, from which I am awakened around noon with a summons from Norman. Shannon's completed round two, and he wants another blonde. Unfortunately, Zen's only blonde at the moment is Shannon, a real blonde, though salon-conducted submissions are fine by him—surprising, since he's so finicky on all other matters of taste.

"What kind of service are you running?" he explodes.

We have a ten-minute back and forth, with me trying to squeeze in a few words on behalf of the stunning brunettes, Cheyenne and Mariko, neither of whom he has seen. Norman explains, as he has many times in the past, that he is a perfectionist. An escort service with a single blonde is improperly managed, as are numerous corporations in which he owns stock, and if he were in charge of Zen or IBM, they would be run efficiently on sound management and marketing principles he has devised by his extensive reading in scholarly business journals.

He decides to call another escort service he's certain will have a bumper crop of girls with hair the color of ripe oats. I call Mariko, tell her things are wobbly, and ask her to keep the night open. Same with Cheyenne, who is perturbed that I woke her earlier in the morning, followed by this call asking for her patience. "I'm going to a play tonight," she announces curtly.

"Could be after that, if not it'll be a thousand for a few hours during the play that will play on."

"It's the last night."

"Going with the flame in the fire department?"

Cheyenne laughs. "Yes. Call me later, and we'll *play* it from there."

Always quick on the comeback, Cheyenne is by far Zen's sharpest razor. She really did graduate from college, her degree in French a bonus for one client, a big player in the New Wired World, who starts his evenings with dinner at Le Colonial or Fleur de Lys, where Cheyenne's delicious low voice skillfully negotiates the menu for both of them. In the solemnity of the dining room, the subdued light casts a sheen on her thick brown hair down to her shoulders, a scene calling to mind Emile Zola's remark that the philosophical core of his masterpiece, *Nana*, represents "a whole society hurling itself at the courtesan."

But Nana was a blonde. The blonde still rules for Norman and 90 percent of the average white males in America. They rule along with Old Glory, apple pie, cheeseburgers, and Mom, though Mom is never *that* kind of blonde. So many to choose from: California beach blondes, wholesome Midwestern blondes, dishwater blondes, honey blondes, platinum blondes, and the emerging majority of Republican blonde chatterheads on TV talk shows.

The image of the dizzy dumb blonde prevailed in the 1950s when the very bright Marilyn Monroe captured the nation's attention, along with her grittier rivals, Jayne Mansfield and Mamie Van Doren, neither of whom were dumb but knew how to play the role. While Sharon Stone and other blonde starlets have stabbed the icepick in that image, the breed is not quite extinct. Although her star has somewhat faded, the ultimate dumb blonde Venus award for this generation will likely fall to Pamela Anderson Lee, striding forth out of the ashes of *Baywatch*, the dumbest show ever aired on TV, viewed at its height by a *billion people* all over the world.

Pamela long ago moved on, but she remains the latest of a pack of fluffers in highcut swimsuits and Dayglo kneepads, rollerblading to the rescue of drowning nerds. Never was CPR more titillating. I can't take more than two minutes of *Baywatch* while channel surfing, and never saw the purloined sex tape with her rockstar ex-husband.

But big points for Pamela's complaints about reporters: "They want to interview my breasts."

So here's the fantasy for men seeking a blonde escort: built like the proverbial brick shithouse, alluring blue eyes, hooters from heaven, anorexic waist, tight bottom, flawless golden skin, makes lots of noise in bed, utters nothing more than drivel.

Around two o'clock, Havana returns with a stuffed shopping bag about to explode, dumps it out on the floor, grabs a pair of scissors out of the desk drawer, and furiously snips away the plastic strips on the pricetags. She gives me a quick fashion show, which includes Steve Madden tennies from Nordstrom; bootcut Baby Phat jeans from True, her favorite haunt on Haight; and a pink T-shirt covered with an imprint of a litter of kittens along with the logo "Cosmic Pussies," a last-minute grab from Villains-Vault, a few blocks from True.

She attacks a box of porn films awaiting Flagstone Walker's lethal reviews. She has no great interest in porn. What excites her is an unopened box containing something new. "Dennis would like this one," she groans, handing me one of the DVDs covered with photos of splattered girls, the cutline at the bottom reading, "Drenched in Cum."

She tears off the cellophane on a fresh pack of Export A Ultra Lights, her latest cigarette of choice, the Canadian brand a buck more a pack, but well worth it, in her view, because it's a cut above Marlboro Lights. "Dennis seems obsessed with porn. I don't care if he watches the stuff, but it's like the only way he can get off. It wasn't like that when we first met, but now he needs the shit when we get it on."

"Whoaa, like past tense, it's over, right?"

"Got a lighter?" she asks, fumbling through her purse to no avail.

I search around the desk, the windowsills, spot one near a coffee cup, hand it over. "I had three lighters last week."

She bats her eyes innocently, flips on the lighter. "What I liked about Dennis more than anything else was his cuddling. He loves to cuddle for a long time, more than any guy I've ever met. But then he wants to fuck, so he puts on a porn vid. Gee, what a thrill for me. I'm a cute girl, I work out, I try to look good for him. Why should I have to compete with all these porn sluts?"

"Revolting, I'd say."

She takes a drag, blows out a cloud of smoke, looks down at the box of DVDs on the floor and gives it a kick. "The whole thing turned out to be so one-way, me always trying to please him. What's worse than the porn is the chatline. That thing costs fifty cents a minute. I saw the phone bill one time and it was over $500, almost all of it on the chatline. He—"

"Uh, is that a line for meeting somebody, or just dirty talk?"

"Kind of both, talking to strangers, saying things you can't say to your girlfriend or boyfriend, sex fantasies and shit, but maybe for a connection too. Anyway, he spends all that money on the chatline and won't take me out to dinner at a nice restaurant, saying he's broke. I know that's a lie and then he says he's broke 'cause I'm leeching off him."

"Okay, but I'm still confused—he's in bed with you, watching porn *and* talking on the chatline. The girl on the phone, uh, she does the 'my pussy's tighter than a pitbull's jaws and I want you to rip it open with your huge throbber right now' bit or what?"

"Hmmm, sometimes, but mainly he wants that because I won't talk dirty to him. That's the one thing I can't do. I've tried, and it just comes out phony. But everything else he gets. I give him all the sex he wants, whenever he wants it—"

"Please, baby, please—that's the problem! You gave him sex whenever he wanted it, but the fucker strangled you."

I get a quart of orange juice and a bottle of Jones berry lemonade, Havana's favorite drink, out of the fridge. Jones knows how to grab the young soda drinkers. Got a picture of a guy on a skateboard on the bottle, and the fine print on the label says soda with "no hidden meanings, no billion dollar ad campaign."

I hand the bottle to Havana. She sits down in the tall task chair, curves her legs underneath it. "That's what I don't get. How can a guy strangle a girl when she never says no to sex? That includes blow jobs in the morning whenever he feels like it, which is most of the time. I don't mind at all, and a lotta girls I know complain about that."

I pour orange juice into a paper cup, my hand steady, which pleases me. "You are every man's dream. Amazing how much work a guy will accomplish nine to five with a knob job before coffee and scrambled eggs. If economists ever had enough sense to investigate this, I'm sure they would find astounding gains in productivity based solely on fellating. In fact, I'm sure the future of the American Empire rests on this alone."

Havana thrusts both her arms in the air, pop bottle in one hand and cigarette in the other, accentuating the victory sign. "Hey, that means I'm a super patriotic American," she yells while I'm taking a swig of OJ. I choke on it, spit some out, and croak, "For sure, the blow job is the true meaning of the Declaration of Independence."

She laughs, reaches over, and crushes her cigarette in an ashtray sitting on the window ledge. She stares out the window for a moment, pushes off the floor with her feet, tucks her legs up, and spins around in the chair.

I watch this blindingly beautiful woman revolving under the light of the afternoon sun, wondering what ticks in Dennis's brain. There he sits in his half-million-dollar house, his contaminated eyes staring blankly at a porn DVD on the five-grand wall-size flat TV, his life with Havana broken beyond fixing, still worshipping her, or what I fear more, his terrible thirst waiting to lay siege on his little fuck doll. "You can't talk dirty, so he needs that on the chatline, plus the porn to jack him up."

Havana stops spinning in the chair, goes into more detail. "Most of the time he just wants to try and impress the girl on the phone, get her to like him so she'll come over. Christ, when he gets on the chatline, I just lose all interest. Makes me feel like shit, and I just want to cry. He starts blabbing away to some girl, then wants me to talk to her, wants *me* to get her to come over for a threesome, since he can never pull it off. One time I did it, just to please him. Actually, she was pretty cool. We kicked it and had a good time.

"All three of us were on the bed fooling around. Every time he put his hands on her, she'd roll toward me. I'm not into girls. God, maybe I should be. I get hit on by girls almost as often as guys. Anyway, she was cute. We kissed a little, that was about it. After she left, Dennis was real upset, said she was more into me than him. But that didn't put an end to it. He keeps pestering me to do it again."

I want to say it sounds like she still loves Dennis, despite her protestations, but say only, "That's the porn—one guy, two or three girls."

Holding the Jones bottle rather absentmindedly, she tips it toward the upended carton of DVDs on the floor. "Yes, sex for him is porn. I'm there to please him. I tried to talk to him about this, let him know there's things I enjoy. Didn't do any good. Gentle strokes and foreplay don't interest him. He's a big guy, sometimes he practically smothers me. Christ, sex with him is like on Animal Planet. Couple a times, when he was pestering me to do another threesome, I said I would if I could also do it with him and another guy. He won't even consider it! I tell him that's a double standard, and he just says that's the way it is."

I lower my voice, drag out the words. "Yeah, but you want a *menage à trois* with two gay boys."

She twirls in the chair again, laughs. "Maybe I should run an ad in the *SF Weekly* asking for that."

"You'll get five thousand straight guys calling saying they're gay."

She slides off the chair and begins putting her new clothes back in the shopping bag. "Probably. I gotta go. Troy's waiting for me. That make you happy?"

"Yes. Stick with him."

I catch a few afternoon Zs, the cell chirps at 3:15, Norman bitterly complaining about a blonde who arrived from Champagne Escorts with a pint of raccoon mascara smothering her eyes. Worse, he thinks she might have walked off with his Dupont diamond-head gold-plated cigarette lighter.

Without a hint of an apology, he reconsiders the options at Zen's poorly managed firm.

Cheyenne prudently decides to forego the theater in exchange for a new acquaintance who favors pricey French wines. She returns to my office a few hours later with a bottle of Norman's Château Ausone Saint-Emilion Bordeaux and announces with cool self-assurance that her brief tenure at Zen is over.

"It's been an interesting experience, and I want to leave while it still is. If I lose interest and keep going, then I really would be a hooker."

I nod in appreciation. "That's why you'll be successful at whatever you do in the future."

Her eyes, dark with a hint of gold, grow wide. She hands me a gift-wrapped package tied with a red ribbon. I open it and pull out a black T-shirt with inch-high white letters on the front: PIMP DADDY.

We both roar. I put it on. "I'm having lunch tomorrow at John's Grill with my editor at the *Chronicle*. Think she'd be impressed if I show up wearing this?"

"That's a sure way not to be successful at the newspaper. She-editor, huh? A lesbian?"

"You got a one-track mind. Femme, but not lez."

"How would she react if you got busted and she found out?"

"Think of the worst punishment an angry butch dyke with a tattoo of Himmler on her shoulder could unleash."

Cheyenne bends at the knees, sweeps her hand, palm down, right to left in a straight line a few feet from the floor. "Better keep low."

"That I'm doing."

She glances around the office. "This is a great spot, even though it's in the middle of drug central. I'll always remember it. I've decided to leave San Francisco. Too damn expensive. I'm moving to Albuquerque. Did you know it's the lesbian capital of the country?"

"Guess I never mentioned it, but yes, I lived in Sappho City, near the university. Great neighborhood. Ten thousand lesbians and twenty thousand cats."

"So I've heard. That's going to be my first stop on the apartment search," she says, moving to the window and taking a last look at the unhappy street below.

"Do you know why so many lesbians live in Albuquerque?" I ask.

She turns away from the window, looks at me. "Nobody seems to know."

I leer at her, piglike. "It's all those big phallic cacti."

She laughs, backs toward the door with a small bow. "A perfect exit line, so I can remember how bad you are." She moves into the hallway, waves, and calls in a childlike voice, "Bye, daddy."

I drink a few beers while waiting for Mariko to return on the last train. I chain-smoke and worry about what I'm doing. Cheyenne opened a door I try to keep closed. The name on the door—or rather, the cubicle at Fifth and Mission—is Lynn Myers, Deputy Editor of the "Insight" section. That's the number two spot, and that's plenty of clout for placing stories by a freelancer with a skimpy journalistic track record. Were it not for her, I strongly doubt the *Chronicle* would run my stories, or certainly not as many as it does.

Several other editors and subeditors in the newsroom labyrinth rummage through mountains of stories, trying to produce a lively and serious balanced weekly wrap-up for "Insight." The credit line on my stories read "Bob Armstrong is the editor of *Exotic*, a San Francisco adult entertainment magazine" until *Exotic* folded. I'm certain editors at most newspapers around the country would not accept stories from a freelancer in journalism's sewer, despite the fact that almost none of my stories have anything to do with the sex industry. The *Chronicle* doesn't seem to care if one of their free-lancers is preoccupied.

But an escort service? I can't tell Lynn Myers about that. We've come to know each other, we're friends, we talk about our lives as well as the news biz. Although I'm not an employee of the *Chronicle*, I do work for her. I worked for several women managers when I was a book salesman. May the glass ceiling shatter. I have no idea why women make better managers and editors, but they do.

I'm looking forward to lunch with Lynn, yet I know when it is over I'll leave John's Grill with a sense of loss, the secret still hidden.

NINE

ariko returns from Norman's Zen party during the midnight hour. Usually happy-go-lucky, her grim face says otherwise. "You're not going to believe what happened."

"After golden showers, I'll believe anything."

"I know Norman, but he didn't know I worked for an escort service."

"I don't believe it."

She collapses in the swivel chair, a flash of narrow almond leg appears beneath a slit skirt. I get a couple of beers, hold one out in her direction. She pouts. "Do you have any wine? I don't like to mix the two, and Norman is really into wine."

I open a bottle of Chianti, pour it in a plastic cup. "This is a big step down from his $200 French vapors, the presentation too. I suppose he has nice wineglasses."

She hoists her cup against my beer bottle in a toast. "Oh yeah, wineglasses light as a feather. He does have good taste, wears beautiful suits and spills red wine and white powder all over them. Total yuppie fuck, but a pretty good-looking guy."

"Consensus there, Havana and Shannon agree. Kind of a moot point for Cheyenne."

"When you told me his name was Norman, I almost asked his last name. But then I figured in a city this big it couldn't possibly be the same guy. I don't know him real well. I met him a couple of weeks ago at a nightclub. He asked me out to dinner. I said how about Rubicon, to scare him off. He said eight P.M. tomorrow night, and then turned around and left, which I thought was smooth as hell. He really laid it on at dinner. I saw the check, over $300. But his true colors came out. Blab, blab, blab. Arrogant. Rude as shit to the waitress, and I hate that, 'cause I've been there."

The tall slender Santa Fe knockout is pissed, her slightly elongated jet black eyes wild as a warrior's. Long black hair licks at the dark golden flesh of her neck, her pulpy mouth shaded with only a trace of lipstick. Mariko's mother is a Pueblo Indian; her father a tall, blue-eyed Anglo, as they say in New Mexico. Like Havana, her lineage only partially reveals the secret consummated in mixed blood. Maybe some Asian? Part Hispanic? Not many outside the rez could make the call.

"After dinner, Norman asked for my phone number. I told him my cell just got disconnected, and gave him my e-mail. He blabs on e-mail too. I answered a couple of them, kind of leaving him some room, even though I don't really want to see him. I can tell you what girls never tell guys. With guys like that, who obviously have a lot of money, do you lose 'em or use 'em?"

"Easy choice for Zen."

She takes another small sip of wine, sets the nearly full plastic cup by the CD player. "Yes, that's straightforward, sex for money. But in real life it's, well, sort of like, uh, negotiation."

"So sending you there blew the negotiation."

"Kind of, but I don't know why I even care. When he opened the door, we both stood there in shock. I almost turned around and left, but I wanted to explain the situation to him. We laughed about it at first. I drank some wine and did a few lines. The living room's all trashed out. Empty bottles of wine and plates of food scattered everywhere, some on the floor. Then he gets all sympathetic about the way I'm destroying my life. We got in a big argument. I told him it was nobody's business what I did. He said, 'I see why you don't want people to know what you're doing.'"

"You could have told him the same thing."

She snaps her fingers. "Wish I had. But I did lie, said when I escort, all I do is give the guys a strip show. He stands up and takes off his shirt and pants, starts dancing around in his underwear, giving me all this crap about 'I-only-dance, sure right.' He pulls his Rips down on one side and says, 'Don't I have a nice ass?' I said yes, but real sarcastic."

"Rips, eh? Tighty whities for the gay boys spreading into the mainstream."

Mariko shoots a pointed finger toward my Versace pants.

"Straight guys should wear nice undies too. Norman does get that. While he's dancing he asks me for a strip show. So I do it. Both of us prancing around kind of got things back under control. Then he wants to fuck me. I said no. I just wasn't going to do it with that asshole. We argued about that for a while. Finally he said he was tired and just wanted to go to bed. I was there for three hours. He gave me $300. I didn't say it should be a thousand, since I didn't fuck him. I smiled, thanked him and left."

I do have an ounce of sympathy for Norman. He reprimands her, knowing she lied about only dancing. After three Zen dolls and one somewhat blonde Champagne Nightmare have passed through his door, he's upset a woman of Mariko's character has morphed into a slut bucket. She's in his living room drinking his Saint-Emilion Bordeaux and snorting his cocaine. He envisions her hosing the entire U.S. Marine Corps, but she won't put out for him. And he still has to pay.

I tell her $300 is fine under the circumstances. "He only wanted to fuck because you wouldn't. With guys, coke cranks it up for some and turns it to jelly for others, like Norman. So would you have hit the hay with him for a grand if you'd known it would be a limp stick?"

Mariko taps her fingers on the arms of the chair for a few moments. "I don't know. Right now I'm not totally broke. If I didn't have a dime, I probably would have."

My tweaked mind wonders: Is it prostitution if the escort knows the encounter will be with an unagitated penis? Even the straight-out fascist feminist Andrea Dworkin would permit a man to enter the vagina, as long as his penis is not turgid.

• • •

After a good night's sleep, I feel steady and alert, awaiting Lynn Myers in the foreboding air of John's Grill. She has a story in mind, but hasn't told me what it's about. She enters the restaurant with a triumphant stride engagingly combined with an editor's studied carelessness. The place is crowded, but we're seated immediately. A young muscular waiter with large dark eyes and shiny black hair approaches our table. "Ah, Ms. Myers, delightful to see you."

She introduces me to Bashar, they chat briefly, and she asks him if his mother has arrived from Istanbul. "Yes," Bashar replies, "and despite the long delay, I'm pleased to say the Immigration Service officials were very helpful."

"Wonderful," Lynn says with a little flutter of her right hand.

Bashar asks if we'd like a drink. I do, but say, "Just a cup of coffee," caving in to the repressive social apparatus fueled by the American media elite that has nearly wiped out the noon martini. The moment Lynn hears the word "coffee," I notice a faint twitching in her lower lip, and a spark of blue exploding behind her mutinous eyes. "Pinot Noir," she says matter-of-factly.

I quickly reconsider, go for Merlot, set a slice of sourdough on a small plate, and make a mental note not to wipe out the bread basket too fast. Bashar takes our order, and we get down to business. Seems there's been a minor crisis among the "Insight" crew, a small group of editors and reporters who have managed to avoid the usual squabbles and backstabbing endemic to any office environment.

Lynn tells me a new editorial assistant, Heidi Swillinger, stirred up an old argument around the water cooler, complaining about the boorish behavior of men despite the gains in the women's movement. In particular, she had told Lynn of an incident at a birthday party for a real estate magnate held at a mansion in Sea Cliff where a profligate minor politician had offered Heidi some inside scoop. The politician (known behind his back as The Pouncer) whetted Heidi's appetite over wine and canapés amongst the crowd of high rollers, wonkers, PR hacks, and city zoning officials. He told her a rival politician had recently signed off on "some interesting real estate transactions" in Millbrae, close to a proposed BART station on the new link to the airport.

He suggested it would be better to give her the full details in private. Smelling a conflict of interest if not outright bribery, Heidi followed The Pouncer up the winding staircase to the library.

"Heidi's favorite author is Thackeray, I mean William Makepeace Thackeray—Heidi always uses his full name," says Lynn, raising her eyebrow significantly. "Heidi walks around the library and notices a complete set of Thackeray's novels in a lovely blue leather binding. She skims through a few of them, notices the bindings are in pristine condition, obviously never read, which disturbs her.

"She puts the books back, turns around and sees her, uh, source, standing behind a couch. He pats the seat, says 'come sit down.' They sit next to each other, and he puts his arm over the back of the couch."

I finish a sip of wine, speak darkly over the rim of the glass. "Hmm, The Pouncer after prey."

"Heidi said that although his hand didn't touch her, she felt his 'hand' "—severe quotation marks fly off Lynn's forefingers— "'growing larger.' "

I gasp at this shocking revelation. Bashar appears, places an appetizer of feta cheese and olives before us. As he walks away, I notice Lynn's eyes following the lustful Turk.

"Heidi's source starts talking about this and that, but nothing about the real estate deal. When she tries to steer the conversation that way, he leans toward her and whispers in her ear, 'We could get into it,' then he pulls back and says, 'in quarters even more private than this. My place?'"

Lynn chuckles mirthfully, raises her wineglass. "Heidi stormed out at that point."

We nibble on the remains of the feta, most of which I have consumed, drink from our wineglasses, mine almost empty. I'm wondering about the exact moment The Pouncer retreated from Heidi's ear. "Did Heidi say with certainty he drew back immediately after saying 'we could get into it'?"

Lynn's eyes light up like a jackpot on a slot machine. "Why, of course. After all, he is a politician, leaving the 'it' hanging there, covered with a figleaf of ambiguity."

I smile lewdly. "*Chron* gonna blow the whistle on him?"

"The file is growing, a few instances with other women in the rumor mill similar to Heidi's. But no grabbing. Not really enough to go public yet. Heidi agrees with that."

The proud son of the Ottoman Empire steps quietly forward, sets down our lunch plates. Lynn intensely studies the ring on his hand like it's the Maltese Falcon. She tells me that Heidi had voiced her complaints about The Pouncer and the whole catalog of men's rude behavior at an "Insight" staff meeting. Jim Finefrock, the editor of the section, was sympathetic to Heidi's point of view on The Pouncer, but felt she too easily denigrated other men for trifling matters. Wanting to lighten things up, he laughed and said, "It's the old question men are still faced with: What do women really want?" Heidi immediately shot back, "What do *men* really want?"

Lynn casts a satisfied smile. "I jumped in and said, 'Heidi, that's a good idea for a story.' Several other people at the meeting agreed." She pokes her fork around the crab, shrimp, avocado, mushrooms, and tomato in her salad special, then points the fork toward me. "So I'd like you to write a story on what men really want." She takes a small bite of avocado (not a random choice out of the salad medley, I suspect) and adds, "We discussed this at the meeting and decided you'd be the perfect person to write it, since you edited a sex magazine."

I try to maintain my cool, but this has me in meltdown mode. I'm tempted to say, "Why, yes, and by the way, I'm a pimp, so I *really* know what men want." Instead, I ask her about running a sex bomb in "Insight," the section of the paper requiring sobriety and careful analysis; the weekly wrap-up devoted to screeds against tobacco, debates on prescription drugs, speculation on who will run for president in '08 (Hillary vs. Condoleezza), and the exciting debate on public versus private power that has engaged the attention of so many Americans since Thomas Jefferson invented the light bulb.

"Heidi has shifted our thinking somewhat, and I'm all for livening up 'Insight' as long as the arguments are solid and serious." She sips her wine. I'm curious where the top dog stands.

"Finefrock up for this?"

Placing her wineglass back on the table, her fingers and thumb seem to grip the stem unduly hard. "Not at the outset, but he came around. He also suggested for a balanced picture we should do a companion piece on what women really want. These will get big play. We're going to run them both as cover stories."

She takes a bite of crab followed by a chunk of tomato. I eat some of my pork chop, waiting for her to spill some juicy gossip on why Finefrock buckled before his new editorial assistant. And I'm wondering how Deputy Editor Myers talked her boss into the "Insight" sex bomb. No details are forthcoming and I don't want to press her further on the matter.

But I'm free to speculate.

First, Heidi is a Pet Shop Boys generation feminist; Finefrock an old white guy. He ignores her rather than reprimand her when her rants escalate into a call for hewing off all existing penises. Finefrock has the same attitude toward women as the ghost who looms up before all in John's Grill: Dashiell Hammett's Sam Spade. Like Spade, former investigative reporter Finefrock resists all female temptations, finds the pretty ones like Heidi clever, manipulative, and extremely dangerous. And, like Spade, he holds the view that the less known about himself the better, thus his absence from the Saturday retreat Heidi organized for the entire "Insight" staff to "explore our lives as full human entities, not just newshounds."

Only Finefrock failed to show. Heidi said nothing to him the following Monday, but Stephanie Salter, an "Insight" staffer and the most radical reporter on the *Chronicle*, stormed into his office and witnessed him nibbling on a bonbon that he quickly tried to hide under his desk. Her accusatory finger pointed to the chocolate smear below his lips. "We all know you love those *lady* sinful treats, never touch the Jack Daniels you claim to drink, and had you gone to the retreat, you could have finally come to grips with the girl inside."

This is not to suggest Finefrock is a fool. He knows he has the *power* to shove any story down the memory hole, but he also knows indiscriminate and frequent exercise of his veto will undermine his *authority*. His influence, his credibility, and the respect of his staff flow from his authority; all this is out the window if he is perceived as power-hungry.

So he goes with the flow and tosses in a compromise with the two-story package. And yet, a residue of tension will always remain. Even with the power card removed from the deck, it still boils down to this tragic duel between the top dog and the Pet Shop feminist: Who has the stronger thighs?

That's what I want to ask Lynn, but don't have the nerve.

She notices my wineglass is empty and catches the eye of the busy Bashar, who quickly responds with refills for both of us. "So tell me, Bob, what do you think men really want?"

I ease my fork through the butter and sour cream into the center of the baked potato, withdraw it and set it on the edge of the plate. "It's not just about sex for men, but . . . well, it is mostly about sex."

Her eyes fly open. A shrimp appears uplifted on her fork. "Heidi certainly thinks that."

A direct attempt to move her freelancer into territory beyond Eros. With my fork in the tender center of the pork chop, I trail my knife along the edge of the bone, slice off a piece, allow the fork to swirl in a sea of applesauce. "Men's magazines like *Esquire* and *Details* run stories occasionally on the new man. The idea is to keep ahead of the curve, let their readers know men have to change their behavior and get in tune with whatever current psychobabble is in vogue. Track the new man trends since General George Patton told his troops going into battle, 'When you get home from this war and somebody asks you what you did, you won't have to say, "I shoveled shit in Georgia."' That might be a way of attacking the question: Patton to Kerouac to Iron John."

Lynn nods in smiling acceptance, takes a bite of salad, followed by a stupefying, reckless move. She lifts her half-filled glass and in three long satisfying gulps she eagerly drains the Pinot. A couple of drops shoot out of the glass, stain the sleeve of her silky white Jil Sander wide-collared shirt. She wipes some wine off her cheek with her napkin, but doesn't notice her elegant shirt appears to be decorated with two drops of virgin blood.

"The new man," she says. "I think you're on to something." The dashing waiter arrives. I toss down my wine, hold up two fingers for refills. Bashar acknowledges my request with a nod, clears the table.

"The salad was excellent," says Lynn, her tone of voice, I sense, sending out a small bullet of desire while Bashar returns a smile that seems to warm her heart.

We bat around a few more story angles for a while, drink the third round I ordered. We pass on dessert. I have a double espresso. Lynn seems spellbound by the foaming hot latte set before her by the enchanting waiter.

I discreetly watch her fill out her Visa card receipt, note a generous tip. Departing the restaurant, she's walking in front of me. I watch her glide past the dark-paneled walls of John's Grill into the street of a great shining city roaring about her.

TEN

ack at my office, I figure it must have been a bad day for Sigmund Freud when he asked, "What do women really want?" I have to wonder, what *would* a woman want from a creepy Viennese guy delving into her darkest secrets? And in a drawing room filled with cigar smoke?

Why did Freud never ask, "What do men really want?"

Women want hugs; men want sex. Women want affection; men want sex. After sex, women want to snuggle while men roll over and snore. We have here an indictment of men as one-dimensional creatures mired in a cauldron of lust. We also have a waterbug of truth.

Culprits include the dude who lives to carve notches on his sex rifle, the hosebag like Dennis who abuses Havana, and the subtle charmer a woman finds irresistible, only to discover she's fatally attracted to a narcissist.

What do men really want? A loaded question, aimed at sex served straight up as the only obvious answer. Still, one man with the obvious answer struck gold. He made millions. His fame lasted longer than fifteen minutes. To this day, beautiful pink and tanned young sirens plop down on the geezer's circular bed. Hugh Hefner, playboy prototype, was the New Man of the '50s.

Since then, we've seen the New Man of the '60s proclaiming on the barricades he would "Make Love, Not War" (now there's a two-fer that may never be toppled). The New Man of the late '70s appeared as a quiet, well-read, non-sports, sensitive kind of guy. When his girlfriend found him too wimpy, the New Man refined himself in the '80s into a man who was both caring and strong. Sports, too. But kayaking, not football. In the '90s, Robert Bly's New Man, Iron John, discovered sensitivity toward women wasn't enough. He needed to dig deeper, return to his primitive origins by drumming in the woods to root out his inner pig.

Guys probably are more sensitive and soul-searching nowadays. No means "no," and it's wise to re-examine conduct around the water cooler. Some do stick by their mate, heap flowers on a woman's bed, leave the toilet seat down. "Supportive," "sharing," and "her space" roll off his tongue. Three drinks a week, two cats, one woman, no smoking.

Still, a problem remains. Before a guy can become a New Man of the Millennium, he must reflect on his identity. That is, he must struggle with the burdens he shares with other New Men. Problem is, most men, New and Old, could care less about their identity. Like George W. Bush, men look in the mirror to comb their hair, not explore their psyches. The last thing they want is a shrink or a paperback off the Gender Studies section at their local bookstore. Why probe the interior of the heart when you can spend the time fly fishing?

Much research has already been compiled on the current New Man. What a bummer. Turns out, he doesn't know what he really wants because he doesn't even know who he is.

His traditional role as provider is diminished, as women enter the workplace in greater numbers. The New Man is dysfunctional, filled with anxiety, inner emptiness, and repressed rage. His sense of self-esteem is shot. Three out of four alcoholics are male.

All the New Men—from the '50s playboy to the latest beaten-down creature—are, of course, caricatures. Yet they give a glimpse of men's changing roles. Who is best equipped to understand the male mind and discover what men really want?

Women, natch.

Feminist thinkers, in a new wave critical of their older Trash & Bash sisters, have turned their attention to men. The New Man is diminished (Naomi Wolf), stiffed (Susan Faludi), emasculated (Camille Paglia). Even Doris Lessing, one of the early feminists in the old school pantheon, points out that "men seem to be so cowed they can't fight back, and it's time they did."

Paglia, in one of her usual provocations, offers some hope for the restoration of male power. Reviving the ancient evacuation myth, she blurted to an interviewer, "Male urination really is a kind of accomplishment, an arc of transcendence."

Paglia confirms Freud's conjecture in *Civilization and Its Discontents* that "primal man had the habit, when he came in contact with fire, of satisfying an infantile desire connected with it, by putting it out with a stream of urine. . . . The first person to renounce this desire and spare the fire was able to carry it off with him and subdue it for his own use. By dampening down the fire of his own sexual excitation, he had tamed the natural force of the fire."

Knowing this, I now find every trip to the urinal sublime, although I still wonder: When is taking a piss just a piss? More important, what of the other side of the equation? Freud goes on to say "women had been appointed guardian of the fire which was held captive on the domestic hearth, because her anatomy made it impossible for her to yield to the temptation of this desire."

But women have come a long way, baby. As Havana demonstrated with her golden shower.

In any case, this stream of thought from Freud to Paglia has my confidence soaring. I can now answer the question. Beyond all the New Man caricatures and roles, what a man really wants pops up now and then in his daydreams. It's a daydream that could come true, but almost certainly won't, making the dream all the more appealing. He does not obsess about it or worry about it. He can't strive for it, work for it, or buy it.

Men want to be heroes.

They want to swoop down like Superman and save the city, dive into the waves and pull out the kid about to drown. The ultimate test? Combat. Men decorated in war, however, are not trying to be heroes; they're usually trying to save their comrades. (Or in my undecorated case, get out alive.)

The proof of this assertion—that men truly, madly, deeply want to be heroes—rests in a pack of lies. Lots of bogus heroes out there. In his book *Stolen Valor*, B. "Jug" Burkett exposed more than 1,750 cases of fraudulent grenade-slinging heroic tales from Vietnam— and those were only the cases Burkett found documented in newspapers.

A guy claims he's got five Purple Hearts and a Silver Star, and the reporter buys it without checking it out. Andy Rooney, who does his homework, once did a *60 Minutes* piece on World War II vets who falsely claimed they'd won the Medal of Honor.

The heroic dream also leads back to the starting point: sex. The knight slays the dragon and rides off with the maiden.

Deep down inside, however, I believe what men and women really want is the same: loyalty. Wanting this is easy. Both men and women falter along the way, but men are more prone to cut and run. At the same time, men mock the woman who bolts from his house, kid in tow, so she can "find herself." For men, the flight seems perfectly justifiable: time to hit the road.

On this matter, my own credentials are nauseatingly impeccable. I have spent my life moving through a dozen different cities like a fugitive, for I am among those who set off anew, float here and there on the winds of chance, and always end up in the same place. This began in my late twenties, while living in Portland. I was itching to bolt. But leave Oregon? Absurd.

My insatiable appetite for any blouse unbuttoning had escalated to the point where I felt trapped in a coil of ruttings, yet never enough ruttings, my subtle charms not always drawing into orbit the woman I had in mind.

You can coolly draw up a long list of reasons for dumping a woman, then tear your hair out when you get dumped. Either way, in the early '70s the deluge of the still single and more often the recently split or divorced spilled into the Chocolate Moose, my favorite watering hole near the Burnside Bridge and around the corner from the current hotspot, Dante's, owned by the publisher of *Exotic*, Frank Faillace. The magazine's office is on the floor above the inferno, so on occasional trips to Portland my past sex life and my current sex career are wonderfully fused.

Speed now, booze then. The Chocolate Moose's deep red interior with a low ceiling ensured the old wooden booths would be filled with clouds of cigarette smoke, a delightful Gomorrah where I surrounded myself with a growing network of friends from grade school, high school, and the University of Oregon, who fortified my craving for approval. The Moose was the hotspot for Portland's future establishment. Lawyers, journalists, architects, artists, teachers, shrinks, and liberal politicos floated in and out, most of us closing in on thirty, carousing and drinking till two.

A few older men inhabited the joint too (rarely older women). They provided us with an airtight defense for enjoying without worry the gold pourings from a bounteous pitcher. Nothing was more absorbing than watching these guys collapsing around us, pickled beyond recognition, broadcasting their secret grief to anyone who would listen. *They* were the pie-eyed alcoholics riddled with the wammies and the DTs. We had it under control.

But eventually I began to see in their bloodshot eyes my own. And more. Too much booze, too many friends, dark grief, confusion, lost laughter in the faces of women. I needed to disentangle myself from all those who had woven themselves into my life. Solution: *RUN.*

Hard to leave Oregon. Knowing rough justice was at work provided some consolation. Ever since the 1848 Gold Rush turned sour, Oregonians have complained about the barbarians from California and elsewhere invading their turf. Most of the barbarians I'd met at the Chocolate Moose were nice Jews from New York and L.A. Don't they deserve a patch of ground in the chosen forest? Mustn't some of us who grew up there give way?

And yet, when you're a native and you light out of Portland on the run and you see the steel bridges over the Willamette River recede in the distance, you feel like the last flower picked up in the sweepings after the Rose Parade.

ELEVEN

D o you have twins?"

What's up with this guy, I wonder, tranced out at the Oxygen Bar, trying to clear my brain from a speed overload with tangerine aromatherapeutic air. "Uh, no, but I have two Asian girls who look like twins." He hangs up.

My Asian dewdrops, China and Saigon (Zen favors geographic names) could pass for twins in a pinch, despite blossoming off different flowers in San Francisco's multicultural garden.

China won't be around for long. Zen is a quick revenge trip for her after numerous fights with her boyfriend. She keeps bird-dogging on him with other guys, returns to his apartment when the sun comes up, gets accused of wanton transgressions. "I'm tired of his crap, so I'm going to whore for a few weeks, then the next time he starts in on me, I'm going to say, 'right, asshole, I *am* a whore.'"

Saigon's twenty-two, looks sixteen, and that's about when she got into the trade. Like Shannon, she's following in the footsteps of her mother, who managed to get into this country after the war. Mother worked in a massage parlor in the Tenderloin, married a white guy whose body had fallen under her strong hands, gave birth to Saigon—then, with citizenship in the bag by way of her loving betrothal, she left her husband.

Every time I see Saigon, I blow back to that afternoon in the Tiger Bar, wonder what might have happened to the French-Vietnamese girl cursed by her mixed blood to remain a stateless person in her own country.

Saigon has had a rough run, though she says working as a joygirl improved after she came to hate sex. "It's dirty, icky, easy to fake, but sex means nothing to me any more." She too may leave Zen soon, having returned to the Catholic church with the possibility of life in a convent. "Nuns do good and have it good. I'd rather have God protecting me than some rich guy wanting to fuck on call."

Given the name, Zen gets quite a few requests for Asians. All the stereotypes play out when men call for them: dreams of the silken-haired geisha girl; the submissive little brown wren giggling while sewing on a button; the patter of tiny feet on a man's back; unspeakable contortions of the body wrought by extensive exercise with chopsticks; or the image of a tough/demure girl in combat boots, naked from the waist up, hurling ninja stars at Sylvester Stallone.

I take another hit at the Oxygen Bar, this time a blend of lavender, red mandarin, and frankincense. This is my first experience paying for air. So-so. You shoot it up through a long tube called a "nasal cannula." The word *cannula* sounds like a terrible bodily invasion, but given my meth habit, I'm in no position to argue about oxy lexicon.

I step out the door into a blanket of gas fumes off a filthy flatbed truck stacked high with flattened cardboard boxes on the way to a recycle station. The rank odor of the black fumes clears my head better than the oxygen. As the truck bounces along Valencia, the ambient air is then filled with the sharp smell of spices from the falafels at Ali Baba next door to the Oxygen Bar.

I walk down the street, stop and check out the menu on the wall in front of Herbivore. I consider marinated tofu and a side of roasted almonds in lemon cayenne seasoning as an ideal follow-up to the O. I change my mind. What's the point of going vegan for a half hour when you like the taste of slaughtered cow?

I cross the street and read some agit-prop posted in the entryway of an anti-corporate media clearinghouse that screens radical videos, ATA (Artists Television Access). "We are terrorized into being consumers," announces John Zerzan, who is identified as a "surplus creator and anti-globalist guru."

Of more interest to me is the guru next door to ATA, a *consulta espiritual* at Botanica Yoruba. This is Havana's favorite store. I scan the wall shelved with hundreds of glass cylinder candles embossed with saints who will protect the believers. I pick up a few disks of charcoal for Havana, head for the counter, and notice a bar of soap in a box illustrated with a gagged woman.

I ask the consulta, who is dressed in colorful robes, if this would be a good gift for a woman. "Si, es for washing away demons."

Perfect. Wash away Dennis.

The wise wicca rings up the charcoal and the magic soap, smiles with a twinkle in her eye, and says she's sure my lady would like a few candles for her cleansing. I extend my arm toward a table filled with candles, shrug with ignorance. She selects some for me. "Never blow them out," she warns. "That will break the spell."

I step out into the sunshine and meander along to Muddy Waters café where I top off the oxygen with a buttery warm scone and a double shot of bitter black espresso. The place is almost empty except for a few brooding young anti-globalist exchangers seated around an old wooden table in the back corner fighting wrongs under the café lights. I remind myself to put a check on my cynicism, don't fret over the long march from the nasal cannula to surplus creation, wait patiently for a meatball to call in search of a girl with lips of mischief, which he finally does sometime after midnight, awakening me in the midst of a warm dream—Havana's slender column glowing under the wobbling flicker of Botanica Yoruba's scented candles.

I call the Santeria intern. Her voice mailbox is full, my complaints having gone unheeded about this recurring problem. After a few more "I'm not in right now" messages from other Zen dolls (and one "I'm out with Jupiter taking a walk in the park"—her snarling Great Dane that's always after my left nut), I reluctantly call Bianca. She's on. The educated pudenda is always on.

I call George, the client, back. He asks for her ETA. I say ASAP.

George says, "Okay, get her over here before all the snow falls." I take that to mean before he snorts all his cocaine. I hustle over to Bianca's. She buzzes me in. The rank odor in the entryway from a Dumpster next to the elevator has me begging for the nasal cannula's tangerine blast. I press the black call button, half of it broken off. The rickety cage drops down. Loud whirring and cranking sounds culminate in a thunderous thump. I won't play those odds, bound up three flights to Bianca's door, opened a crack.

I step inside, hear the sound of the shower running, yell out her name. "Just a sec, I'll be right out."

Her studio is a pigsty. Clothes scattered everywhere. Piles of junk pushed into the corners, including a bicycle with a missing wheel. Dirty dishes and coffee cups spill over the counter into a small metal stained sink. I clear off a seating space at the end of a long L-shaped sectional, the centerpiece of her home. A low table in front of the sectional groans under the weight of half-filled coffee cups, day-old 7-Eleven Piña Colada Slurpees, crushed paper cups, wads of paper, CDs, videos, beer bottles, one high-heeled shoe, and an open pizza box containing three pepperoni slices decorated with cigarette butts. Bianca has about a dozen ashtrays, all working at full capacity. I unwad a paper sack, pour the contents of one ashtray in it, sit down, and light up.

A few minutes later, she comes blasting out of the can in a swirl of powder and strong perfume. She's wearing a white blouse, riot green shorts, and yellow sandals with crisscrossed straps running like a spider up her legs. A cig dangles from her lip. I hear a muffled ringing in the bowels of the sectional. Bianca's hands furiously dig under some clothes.

"Keep it short, George is waiting," I say as she extracts her cell.

"Don't tell me what to do," she snaps. "This is my home." She punches the keypad, starts blabbing away. I press my forefinger on one nostril, snort a few times. She ignores the snow cue, keeps talking, then tips her head and crooks the cell between neck and shoulder. One hand snaps open a pocket mirror while the other smears lip gloss across a rounded mouth and pushed out lips, still talking with a slight slur. Superb SF multitasking.

She finally gets off the cell, throws on a long black coat and says triumphantly, "Now I'm ready."

As the gold pile rolls out of the Tenderloin across Van Ness, she asks, "Do you have a gun?"

"No."

"You should. I got a friend that can get you one cheap."

Actually, I do have a gun gathering dust on a closet shelf. But for escorting, I rejected the final arbitrator of disputes on the grounds that it would only make matters worse. I live through every night with a frightening prospect—there is no way to guard a girl in trouble. As a cautionary measure, all escort services have the girl call and check in a few minutes after she meets her trick. That, at least, makes the client aware that somebody knows her whereabouts. And Zen's $500 entry fee likely weeds out serial killers who want to exterminate prostitutes after porking them.

Nonetheless, fear is always in the back of an escort's mind. We all try to resist fear. We fear losing a job or losing a lover. Parents fear for their children, men and women dart their eyes left and right when standing before an ATM in the deep of night. But these fears are fleeting. Escorts always have butterflies in their stomachs when they enter the darkened doors of silent houses.

Sometimes, the girl says her driver is nearby, even if she took a taxi. If she senses the guy is kind of spooky, she might go further, pointing out to him that her driver is large and black. Frequently, the men assume this, or worse—worry an iron-fisted black man lurking in the bushes outside the window will come storming through the door. I've had callers ask for assurance they will be safe. Some have told me they had their wallets ripped off by girls from other escort services. Bad news, but they really should have tucked it away in a drawer rather than leaving it in their pants pocket during the fuck-o-rama, or really dumb, setting a fat one bulging with credit cards on a bedside table near wandering fingers.

I explain to Bianca why I'm not going to pick up the gun. She snottily replies, "Well then, I'll buy one."

I should change the subject, but my mood says escalate. "How are you going to get your gun if he pulls one on you first?"

"I can handle it. I'll push his hand away and kick him in the balls."

"If he's grabbed you from behind and has the pistol stuck in your ear—"

"Fuck you," she interrupts. "Christ, we're on the way to some asshole's house, and I'm the one who has to deal with him while you sit on your butt in the car reading a magazine." She picks up a copy of *The New Republic*, rolls it up and slams it over my head.

"Hey, careful, I might drive off the road."

"You drive like an old lady."

"I drive the speed limit."

"Drive over the speed limit so I can get there before George does all the coke. I need a big fat line," she says as a taxi whips around me.

"For sure you do," I grumble. "I got to your place in plenty of time, sat on my ass for a half hour while you put your face on in the bathroom."

"It was only ten minutes," she yells. (True.) "That's the problem. You don't give a fuck about me." (Also true.) "I'm the one taking the chances. I'm the one who could get killed, and you make it worse by talking about some guy putting a gun to my ear."

She's right. I ease off. "I'm sorry. I only brought that up 'cause you started talking about a gun—"

My apology is useless, which is why I usually don't apologize in an argument like this. She goes ballistic. "It doesn't matter. The only thing that matters is *me*. You're a man so you can't possibly understand what it's like to do what I'm doing."

I don't answer. We drive for a while in silence, pass the VA hospital where I get my monthly allotment of four Viagra pills for only seven bucks. Helps, but my standard isn't as high as I'd like. Sometimes, I toss a couple to Troy by way of Havana ("like all night, it's almost too much for me").

We turn up a dark street near the ocean. I glance over and see the hurt in Bianca's eyes. Then she starts to tremble. A low moan rises from her gut, exploding into a single expletive, repeated endlessly: "Shit, shit, shit, shit," she incants like a Hare Krishna.

She holds up *The New Republic* with both hands, rips it in half, tears out the pages, wads them into little balls and tosses them around the car's interior, muttering "shit" with each random pitch. The last vestiges of liberalism in its pages crumple and fall as we approach a house where a client anxiously awaits something far swankier than *TNR*.

"Guess I'll just smoke for an hour, since I got nothing to read." (A lie.)

"Hope you get cancer," she snarls, gets out and slams the car door shut.

I reach over the backseat and grab a backup book, then pull a flashlight out of the glove compartment. Pitch black outside. Usually, I can park under a streetlight, but pimps who read must improvise and find whatever source of illumination they can.

My favorite spot, the Galleria Park Hotel on Sutter, offers a cozy lobby with a big fireplace. A few weeks back I'd tapped on the Galleria's door during Zen's popular 2/3/4 A.M. range, accompanied by Nikka, a tall raven-haired noirish standout. The night attendant, wearing a dark suit with a red handkerchief in the breast pocket, let us in when I gave him the name of the guest scheduled for service. He eyed us without a trace of suspicion, discretion paramount at San Francisco's nicer hotels.

Nikka's large handbag contained a whip, cuffs, ropes, and miscellaneous S/M accoutrements. Zen rarely gets such request, the wide array of deviants in San Francisco having been busted up into niche markets—straight, bi, lez, swing, TV/TS, fetish, tantric massage (phony), crossdressing, etc. Occasionally, I get a call from some guy who misses the specialty ads in the alternative publications. Nikka fields the state-of-emergency flogging calls.

We whisked up the elevator to see Jackson. I did not meet Jackson, nor do I ever meet my clients. Nikka aggressively advanced down the hallway. I went back down to the lobby, settled in a soft chair by the fireplace with Bret Easton Ellis's *American Psycho.* The Manhattan serial killer was describing his wardrobe—a tweed suit and cotton shirt by Yves St. Laurent, a silk tie by Armani, shoes by Ferragamo.

Close, even had an edge wearing my Liste Rouge custom-made shirt from Paris. I pulled out a pack of Camel Light Wides, set it down on a cherrywood table, contemplated if I should step outside for a fix, knowing the night manager would have to let me back in. Not wanting to push his sense of discretion, I decided to forgo the smoke.

I read some more, looked up at the clock high on the mantel above the fireplace. During the twenty minutes that had passed, Ellis's fashion-forward serial killer had purchased a couple of butcher knives and a bottle of hydrochloric acid for torturing a white rat, preparation for prettier bait.

I put the book down and let my mind wander. I imagine Mistress Nikka flailing away with her whip of choice—a short one with a steel stock and a series of metallic studded knots woven into the calfskin thongs. She stomps around Jackson in knee-high stiletto-heeled boots. He's naked on all fours. She cracks the whip in the air, then slams it down on his soft white butt. He buries his nose in the carpet and begs for more. She delivers a dozen furious blows with the strength of a gladiator. Each cut sinks deeper. His ass looks like a marshmallow in flames as he crawls away and curls up in a corner, burying his face in his hands.

Reaching in her bag, she pulls out a pair of pliers, holds it over his right nipple. An expression of sheer terror sweeps across his face. Nikka's hands squeeze the handle. He screams, bucks, and shoots his wad.

Nikka wipes the sweat off her brow, gives him a light kiss on his forehead. He nods in approval. She snaps the pliers in the air once more. "A San Francisco special," she coos, "call Zen again on your next trip to the city."

Oh, to be by the Galleria fireplace right now, I wish, shivering in front of the steering wheel, waiting for Bianca. I hear footsteps rushing toward the car. I snap off the flashlight, toss it in the back-seat along with the book. She throws open the door and squeals, "George gave me $800, and he's a slammin' guy."

She fills me in at length on George, who is young, tall, shaved head, tats, and just scored ten grand on some kind of computer credit card scam. 'Nuff said.

She runs the eight bills through her fingers, pulls off two. "Got a fifty?"

I take the two bills in my right hand, reach across with my left and snap up another. She tries to grab it back, but I fold it in my fist. "Hey, that's my money," she snarls.

I remind her she owes me $150 from the Night of the Peacock Feather. She whines on about the fact that I haven't called her since then, and says it isn't fair Havana always gets called first. I don't tell her Havana almost always remains incommunicado via her bulging voice mailbox, nor do I mention that the name Bianca is at the bottom of the Zen list.

Then a lucky break: a man calls from San Mateo. Zen loves back-to-back. She's happy. I spin back through town and down the freeway, past the airport hotel signs towering on poles high in the air, their neon Ramada Quality Best Western Marriott Hampton Hyatt Holiday Inn pampering arms calling out Zen-n-n-n-n-n-n in an early morning red taillight ride.

The client lives close to downtown San Mateo. I drop the bitch off, drive over to Fourth Street, and pull up in front of Starbucks just in time for the opening buzz. Only one customer is in the place, a man sitting near the barista action, wearing a gray suit and reading the *New York Times*. I prefer window seating, but after getting my espresso, I sit two tables away from him. With any luck, he'll only stay a few minutes, graciously leaving the paper of record behind. I've found this a common practice at Starbucks. They have a lot of well-heeled addicts who truly believe and *practice* the trickle-down theory.

Bianca calls, checking in, calls back a half hour later, saying the client wants her to stay with him the rest of the day, maybe into the night. While I'm talking to her, the gentleman nearby does the right thing. As he goes out the door, I slide nonchalantly over and snag the Grade-A prime news. Bianca tells me she's got a thou with a good chance more green will flow after the sun goes down. Gotta give her credit. She can reel in the fish.

Turns out I'm the fish.

I don't know if she stayed an hour, or if she's still there. She's gone, the manager of her apartment tells me a few days later. "Ripped me off for two months rent," he adds.

Glad I grabbed that money out of her slimy fingers. Back at the office, mail slipped through the slot sits on the floor: an ad for office furniture, a bill for an overdue parking ticket, a political campaign letter trumpeting Gavin Newsom's grandiose plan to solve the homeless problem, an unsigned form rejection from *The New Republic* on my Britney Spears essay (I'm starting to appreciate Bianca's blasphemous critique of *TNR*), and a postcard from Cheyenne in Albuquerque. "Rented a two-bedroom house near the U for $800 a month!!! Cats everywhere. Dykes, too, one from the fire department. Zen on." I flip it over and smile. A picture of a cactus.

Cheyenne's the only Zen doll who ever contacted me after bailing out. Cordelia did call to let me know she was returning to London. Even that is somewhat unusual. Girls just disappear. I keep calling and get no answer. The formal resignation comes with "this phone number is no longer in service."

Last night, I got Mariko's resignation message and last month Shannon's. Given all the drama with her mother she'd laid on me, it came as a surprise when Shannon simply vanished. I don't know if she left with her mother, or left her mother here in the city to fend for herself. I toss the postcard on the desk and think about Shannon's notepad, her lifeline when she was under eighteen, her black book with names and phone numbers of the sad bastards she'd picked up in the Tenderloin. "The phone is safe," she'd said. "I don't have to be on the street."

She'd sniffed out johns like a hungry wolf awakened by the scent of lambs, removed herself from the reach of the law as best she could. That may seem like an obvious tactic for survival in the combat zone, but most low-rent hot pots are so strung out they can't even get it together to make a to-do list. Shannon was organized, but I doubt she'd ever transfer those skills to a nine-to-five job. She never expressed any desire to get out of the life. But down the road the life will probably get out of her. There's only one direction for old hookers: Down.

I light a cigarette with shaky fingers, snort a line of speed to calm me down, and finish off the book I'd been reading the night Bianca saw George and the San Mateo high roller: Ron Rosenbaum's *Explaining Hitler.* His meticulously researched book moves me to haul out a carton filled with articles and reams of my own notes for my work-in-progress, *Hitler the Toilet,* and toss the pile in the garbage. Depressing in that I'd never be able to come closer to Rosenbaum's achievement; liberating in that I've had the box for years and made little progress on the book. Thanks, Ron, for lifting this weight off my shoulders.

Moreover, after plowing through Rosenbaum's analysis of Hitler's sex life, I'm now persuaded my take on the exterminating pig as a toilet is wrong. The famous golden shower story Otto Strasser claimed he heard firsthand from Geli Raubal seems dubious. The golden shower, along with unsubstantiated rumors of the brown-shirted leader's coprophilic leanings have been seized upon by "psychohistorians and psychoanalysts who had felt that *here* must be the dark, hidden, repressed *truth* about Hitler's psyche," writes Rosenbaum.

Hitler may well have delighted himself with all the twisted fantasies available in the catalogue of sexual perversions, but the dots don't connect between alleged acts of perversion and his desire to gas Jews, gypsies, gays, commies, and "useless eaters." Along with Geli's golden shower, a host of other rumors remain just that—rumors. Hitler's impotent, Hitler's gay, or Hitler contracted syph when he visited a brothel in Vienna to celebrate his seventeenth birthday (all he ate that happy day was a torte, at home in Linz with his mom).

Although it hasn't been made into a movie yet, the contents of Hitler's jelly bag has always been a source of great excitement. The amount of attention given to the one-ball theory, as Rosenbaum says, is almost comic. "The lost testicle has become a repository for hope that some singular solution—an explanatory single-bullet theory—exists somewhere to explain *everything.*"

Rosenbaum traces the one-nutter story back to a line in a popular Army marching song in World War II: "Hitler—has got only one ball." I stumbled across an earlier (probable) one-ball entry on February 29, 1936, by Janet Flanner, the Paris-based correspondent for *The New Yorker:* "There is a rumor that Hitler was wounded genitally in the war."

Hitler was wounded twice and almost blinded by mustard gas in World War I, but there is no evidence in his war record that either of his wounds approached the level of Jake's in *The Sun Also Rises.* That aside, Flanner, a shrewd observer of the human condition, went on to say, "His real abnormality apparently consists of the insignificance of his sexual impulse, probably further deadened by willful asceticism. Emotionally, Hitler belongs to the dangerous small class of sublimators from which fanatics are frequently drawn."

George calls, asking for another round. "Say, man, that Bianca was wild. I was wondering if I could get her phone number. I mean, it was cool, the escort gig, but just a fly. And now I'm broke, but I think she'd like to see me. Are you down?"

"It doesn't work that way," I say, not filling him in on Bianca's flight.

George persists. "Maybe we can deal. I don't have a regular job. I'm not into corporate sackhead fucky-fuck. I work off the black lot. 'Cept for a little thing I ran last week, it's been dry. Maybe I could work for you."

I almost say "I don't hire one-nutters" and click off, but I gotta hear George out. "Do you need any male escorts?" he asks.

My standard response to this frequent query, "Are you gay?" is usually met with a huff, or a firm, "No fucking way!" Plenty of work available for rent boys, but these straight guys are dreaming, thinking women will pay to have sex with them.

The demand for a gigolo is near zero. One woman did call me. "I want a man to scale the wall of my house on a rope, come through the window and ravish me." I'm sure she was putting me on, although I told her I could send Romeo over as soon as he finished poking Juliet. She didn't miss a beat: "Tell Romeo to stay away from that bitch."

Click.

I tell George the only work available is on the Castro shuttle. "I'm not gay, but I could do that," he says.

"Are you bisexual?"

"No, I'm straight. But I'll do anything to make some scratch so I can see Bianca again. If that means sucking cock, I will suck cock."

The power of the skirt, for sure.

TWELVE

harles, Havana's regular, calls wanting some lip dancing on his love truncheon. He's an escort's dream client—mid-forties, generous, mega-rich. He sees her about once a month, loves watching her strip to Tina Turner's dance music, and has recently acquired a taste for E she carefully wraps in pink strips of paper cut out in the shape of stars. She usually stays with Charles a couple of hours, ending her "sessions," as she calls them, sloshing around in his hot tub.

Havana once asked him straight out, "How come a cute guy like you calls escorts?"

Charles told her he sensed most women were only after his money. "For me, paying for it is a freebie, a done deal."

That explains everything. Or nothing.

Amazingly, Havana answers when I call. She's out dancing. I bolt into SOMA, park the gold pile halfway up on an alley sidewalk near the Cat Club, hope it doesn't get towed. I'm in a hurry because

Charles always wants to see her *right now*. He well knows timeliness is foreign to Havana's nature, so he likes to put the pressure on me to deliver. Can't blame him since Zen is far from a freebie.

Inside the Cat Club, I watch a few couples break up their dancing by jumping up and batting candy-colored streamers hanging from the ceiling. One dude blows steadily on a plastic whistle while his girl, hair teased into orange spears—Christ, I hate orange—sticks her fingers in her ears. Another girl with silver paint on her face slides past and disappears into a pack of freestylers. A group of Hispanics work one section of the floor, nodding at each other like something big is about to happen.

I spot Havana dancing with a short guy wearing thick black-rimmed milk bottle glasses. He dances like a robot controlled by some unknown power. I wonder how she heard her cell ring under the steady house music pounding at 120 beats a minute. The trance-inducing drone seems to give everybody the energy of wild horses pounding along the Nevada desert. It has the opposite effect on me, like an electric vampire draining my blood. Havana has a vampire look about her, a slash of purple-black lipstick, black catsuit, and a black eye.

She wheels over and introduces me to her partner with a fitting name, Space. I shake his hand. "I'm Havana's uncle, Space, gotta take her home to keep her out of trouble."

His eyes narrow behind his big specs. "I'm the least of your troubles. I'm a nerd."

I like this guy. "Well, now, we all know that young nerds end up in the ruling class. Very dangerous types on the way up and worse when they get there. You get those glasses off Buddy Holly?"

"Who?"

"Never mind. Look, I hate to be a party pooper, but we really got to split."

Havana gives him a big hug. "Bye, Space, see ya later."

In the car I ask Havana about her black eye. "I don't want to talk about it right now," she mumbles meekly, covering the blemish below her eye as best she can with makeup. Point well taken. I don't want to upset her on the way to see Charles. His house is in Pacific Heights, not far from another house where inside sits the perp who smacked her, eating Hostess Ding Dongs and spewing his jiz at the porn on his wide-screen TV.

At the Zen HQ in the Grant Building, Havana bounces around the room, waving a wad of Charles's money. I listen to her babbling for a few minutes. She's all bubbly and happy. I don't want to bring her down, but I do want to know what's behind the black eye. Turns out she's ready to unload.

Seems the crisis was sparked when one of the speakers on Dennis's stereo went out. "He comes screaming into the kitchen, saying I fucked up his stereo. I was getting some chicken out of the refrigerator. I put it on a plate. He grabs the chicken off the plate, yells, 'That's my food you're eating.' I just stood there stunned. Then he grabs the plate and throws it on the floor. When he gets mad, he does that, breaks things like a little kid having a temper tantrum.

"I told him I was leaving, went into the living room and put on my jacket. He came after me, slapped my face, knocked me down on the floor. Then he jumped on top of me and started strangling me again. I kept screaming, 'No, no, stop it.' Finally, he did. I got up and ran outside. Then he came after me again. I ran down the sidewalk. He got in his car and backed out of the driveway so fast, he bumped into a parked car. I just kept going and caught the bus downtown."

She stands by the window staring out in the darkness. I come up behind her, rub my hand on her shoulder. "I got one question. This is the third time he's strangled you. Three strikes you're out, right?"

"Yes," she says firmly.

I check the time. Ten till three. The bars are closed, but an after hours spot will be even better. "Okay, let's go party where your black eye will shine."

Bordering on SOMA's glitzy turf, the Power Exchange on Otis Street sits in the remains of an industrial area. The four-story concrete building is a sex club. Designed for carnal delights of all orientations, the Mainstation for gays occupies the second and third floors; the Substation for straights takes up the first floor and basement.

No neon sign out front, only two red doors marking the appropriate entrances. The Substation is divided into a series of rooms along with open areas fenced off with chickenwire. Nooks off to the side, a few closet spaces, and a long pitch-black hallway lined with a series of open booths provide semiprivacy. While strip clubs set up bright lights for the peelings, the Power Exchange is deceptively dim throughout.

Inside, the first thing Havana sees is a sign on a steel wall:

SFPD LOCKUP
TO PROTECT AND SERVE

Behind the sign loom four open jail cells. Havana bounces into one of the cells. "This is so-o-o cool."

I run my hand along one of the bars. "I think the owner somehow got the remains of a real jail."

Havana stomps on the cell floor. "I'd like to buy a jail and put Dennis in it for life."

Passing through the cells, I point toward a short staircase leading to a room in a mock hot-sheet hotel. "You might file a complaint with the police department to get the strangulations on the record," I say as we walk up the staircase into the tiny room where a boxspring covered with a leather mat awaits guests. Havana sits on the mat. As it caves in around her, a tranny in a tight red sequined dress appears at the top of the stairs, gives her a warning. "Hey, girl, be careful, that'll swallow you up."

Havana swings her long legs up and stretches out invitingly on the mat. "Pretty comfy, actually."

The tranny moves out of the dimness, her mahogany skin shines on her shoulder a few inches away from a bare 50-watt bulb bolted on the wall. She sashays around me, brushes her hand over my hair. "Such a pretty couple, distinguished gentleman whose gray hair appears dyed and a hotly spiced maybe Asian maybe calypso Trinidad girl, am I close?" she asks, casting a come-hither look at Havana.

"Maybe Cuban on one side and white burb on the other," comes the quick reply.

The tranny's satisfied grin accompanies a fetching hip thrust. "I'd say Cuba won out."

We introduce ourselves. Griselda's dark brown eyes zero in on mine. She asks if we've been here before. I grin. "I have. First time for Havana."

Griselda waves a pointed finger in my face. "Baaaad boy. Maybe you missed something. How about I give both of you a guided tour?"

Tourism seeps in everywhere. Eat at Fisherman's Wharf, swing yourself off the platform of a cable car, or head over to San Francisco's underbelly and scope out the leather chaps over a man's ass bigger than a Ukrainian wheat farmer's. I'm definitely up for Griselda's invitation darkened with a lovely gender-bending smile. "How much?" I ask.

Griselda glowers. "Honey, I charge for *some* matters, but this is free."

I pull a twenty out of my back pocket, press it in her hand. "I respect your integrity, so call this free money."

Griselda blinks, opens her hand and kisses the bill. "I do like Mr.

Jackson." She turns toward Havana, waves the bill. "Ooh, honey, you got yourself a keeper!"

"He's my uncle."

The red dress begins shimmying down the stairs, a follow-me forefinger bending off the right hand. "Uh-huh, sure, and call me Aunt Griselda."

We pass through another room, move into an open area, where a male bottom bent over a sawhorse takes a few resounding whacks from a female top. The S/M scene dominates the Power Exchange, most of the players exceedingly unattractive with a sprinkling of beauties like Nikka, Zen's domina, who frequents the place, but never with her clients. Too undeserving, Nikka says of her human ashtrays. (She likes to flick soot from the cigars she smokes into their mouths.)

Quite a menu at the Power Exchange for a gourmet's curiosity. Coffins for the satiated, gym horses for the very risky, wooden wheels with straps on the sides to secure a victim for a turn of the screw. Canes, paddles, whips, and riding crops for de-spunking the black and blue; clothespins clamped on testes for C&B (cock and ball torture).

Not a lot of butts flaming under whips among the fetish crawlers as we pass through the dungeons. I slide my arm over Griselda's shoulder, whisper in her perfumed ear, "Where's the Lockheed VP bound and gagged with a tennis ball in his mouth, or a naked senator on the cold concrete with a boot planted on his neck?"

She bumps my hip. "Maybe nobody's doing anything 'cause you're here, Unn-cle Bob."

Havana sees a group huddled near the open doorway in the distance, some on their tiptoes looking over a partial wall. "Let's check that out."

"Gawkers in Dockers," mumbles Griselda as we move across the concrete floor. We find an open space by the wall. I can just see over the top. A big guy in black vinyl pants with chains dangling off his belt strides around a naked rail-thin girl with his whip in hand. She's lying face down, tied to a four-poster bed. "What's going on?" asks Havana.

I drop to the ground on one knee. "Get aboard and you'll see." She puts her legs over my shoulders. I push myself up, nearly break my back. Christ, I got to work out more. Havana rests her hand on top of the partial wall and looks down on the action. I hear the whip come down and hear Griselda behind me. "Call Uncle Bob for a rough, tough ride."

I ease down, Havana slides off. She's 5'4" at 105. Griselda's trim, about 5'8", 130 or so. I don't know if I can handle her, but feel compelled to ask. Maybe she saw me wobbling. In any case, she declines. "Been that. Done there."

We saunter back through the dungeons. A stick man a couple inches taller than me decked out in black leather swings past. Griselda waves her long red-clawed nails toward him. "Hi, love," he says, moves on, stops here and there, says a few words to everyone like a politician working a fundraiser. "Harris is real old leather, one of the first into S/M way back. Throws parties at a warehouse so he's here a lot working it."

I glance at Harris, who's scrutinizing the Power Exchange's princess of the night, a young honey in jackboots, hip-hugging pants decorated with eight-inch safety pins, long purple tresses sprouting through black hair. She has a relaxed, self-aware leave-me-alone stance. Harris appears to get that message, wisely spins on his heel and moves on.

We stop in front of an angelic black girl tied to a cross, crucifixion-style, blindfolded with a red headband. A white guy walks around her, stroking her with a huge feather. "I'd go for that," says Havana.

"Whip too?" asks Griselda.

"Maybe, not too hard, though."

"Never done S/M, huh?"

"No, but I'm open."

"Bottom, not top, right?"

"Yeah, I'm the submissive type. I mean sex-wise. But that doesn't mean I can get pushed around. I got balls when I want to."

Griselda roars. "Don't we *all*, girl!"

Havana embraces Griselda. After a deep hug, Griselda slaps Havana's ass. "Head-wise a bottom, and a bottom to die for. Bet old Uncle Bob can't get enough of that innnn-cest."

"Definitely," I say.

Havana hugs Griselda again. "It's been great, but we gotta go. Bob's up much later than usual. He needs some sleep."

"Come by again. Next time, all three of us can play in the hot sheet hotel."

Havana gives her a thumbs-up. "I'm game."

Griselda's finger lightly touches Havana's face below her eye. "Makeup can't cover up a black eye. Uncle Bob?" she asks, a disbelieving tone in her voice.

"No," I say. "Her boyfriend, whom I would like to kill."

Griselda pokes me in the chest. "Would? *Should.*"

She turns away, a red dress evaporating in the universe behind a dark boundary she so delightfully smashes.

THIRTEEN

I t's only a matter of time before Richard May paints himself out of his apartment, the walls of his dingy studio covered from floor to ceiling with paintings, recent work bolted on top of previous efforts, sometimes three or four deep. Many of the frames shoot off at different angles, so on one wall a slash of red on a large trapezoidal painting peeks out from under a slightly smaller rectangular work; on another wall, four various-shaped frames stacked on top of each other form a luminous geometric block of chopped-up colors in rows of parallel lines. Sometimes he'll sabotage his hard edges with a blast of speckled paint or overlays of wire, but pure form is his game.

The landlord of the Tenderloin dive on Ellis Street provides some relief, the hallway on Richard's floor a dark venue lit by sixty-watt bulbs overhead, the rambunctious rhythm of his growing special exhibition careering all the way down to the window where three large trash containers cover the emergency exit.

Richard has a hundred canvases or so stored in a barn in Montana where his former weed supplier lives. The promising painter made a good living in the pot business for about ten years, then decided it would be best to get out before he got popped. Now it's nine to five on an administrative job with painting at night and on weekends. He's also got paintings stashed in friends' closets all over town, a half dozen at my office behind a bookcase, in addition to the Doors of Perception on the wall.

Richard's never had a gallery show, nor has he made any attempt to do so, though I think his highly structured abstracts are better than most of the stuff I see in cafés and bank lobbies. Piet Mondrian, Barnett Newman, Kenneth Noland, Ellsworth Kelly, and Frank Stella influence his work, though Stella less so. "I don't do circles," he says, which I find amusing, as though a circle is a dangerous drug.

Richard's flipping through an art book I brought over, *Mirroring Evil: Nazi Imagery/Recent Art,* highlights from an exhibit at the Jewish Museum in New York. These works of art invite the viewer into the world of the perpetrators' propaganda and machinery of death: a concentration camp built with Lego blocks, a collage mixing pictures of nude women with Nazi officers, a photograph of one of the artists holding up a can of Diet Coke superimposed on a grainy image of camp survivors.

"You should try biting off the Third Reich," I suggest. "Paint a fifteen-foot pink swastika. Better yet, a whole series of distorted, twisted, broken-up swastikas, maybe a rainbow-colored multicultural swastika. Some gallery would go for it, figuring the art critic at the *Chronicle* would jump all over it."

Richard balks. "What you are suggesting is not art. That's just using art to get attention. That's what these guys are doing," he says, closing the book. "An artist striving to get to the truth would never do that."

"Couldn't you have it both ways? I'm sure some of the artists were just doing it for the attention. But not all of them wanted to turn the ovens of Auschwitz into a comic book. Their works could be considered a strike against a tyranny that's long dead, yet never seems to go away. The pink swastika could be seen in that light. Wouldn't that be striving to get to the truth while at the same time recognizing that it might also get your paintings in a gallery?"

Richard smiles, shakes a finger at me. "Sounds kind of slippery. Truth through the back door. Any artist could do what you're asking, so why would you want me to do it?"

"I don't think any artist could. You're the perfect candidate, 'cause you're an abstract expressionist. The swastika fits right in, no matter what its meaning."

Richard picks up a pencil, draws a few lines on a piece of scratch paper, a swastika with a diagonal line through it, like a no-smoking sign. "The swastika is an ancient symbol found in many cultures." He pauses, makes a concession. "If you strip away any social or political significance, the swastika is as close as you can get to the perfect form, the square and the circle being perfect forms."

. . .

Walking through the Tenderloin after I leave Richard's studio, I feel uneasy, bumming him out with my Nazi feast. I've known Richard for a long time. His background would not foreshadow a future as an artist. He grew up in a tough neighborhood in the Bronx, but avoided the lure of the gang world. He dropped out of high school, turned it around later and graduated from college with a degree in economics. Later, he turned to painting, just as I turned to writing.

On Jones Street, I see a few listless figures spill out of a bar about to close for the night. Dazed and drunk, they crash along the sidewalk, one guy stopping in front of the iron gates of an apartment building where he punches all the buzzers and walks on. Another dude slumps down on the sidewalk, cradling in his arms a bottle of wine in a brown paper bag like it's a baby. A few burnt-out junkies sitting on the sidewalk split a bag of Oreos and share a quart of chocolate milk.

A hooker down the street waves at a boat-long white limo passing by. The limo slows, zooms away. She flicks her cigarette butt at the limo, climbs up the steep street, grows tired at the end of the block, rests her eyes on me. "Wanna date?"

"Can't afford it tonight," I say, though I have no interest.

"How much money ya got?"

"About three bucks."

She sighs, rolls her eyes back into two deep sockets competing with pitted areas of skin on her face. "Ya got an ATM card?"

"No," I lie.

"Got a check?"

That takes me aback. "Yeah, but I don't think you'd want it."

"Honey, I'm not some asshole at the Check Mart. I'll take your check."

"Thanks, but not tonight."

Back at the office, I drink a beer and think for a long time about her burnt-out world. She'll get some traffic, plenty of horny midnight ramblers circling through the Tenderloin. The corner girl dominates the scene for several blocks just by her presence. Leaning against the wall, a slight wave of the hand, the movement of her lips, a sexy street pantomime, a wandering eye piercing the night. The hunting eye, steady, straight, zeroing in on her target like a sniper. But it's not "one shot, one kill," more like a million spent shells and nothing to show for it.

Back at the office, Havana calls at four in the morning. "I'm downstairs. Can I come up?"

Down the marble staircase of the Grant and back up the stairs with her, since both elevators await the Otis man's expertise, an occasional problem for all who rent offices in this fine old building. We endure the challenging elevator, no hot water in the restroom sinks and junkies' needles in the toilet stalls in exchange for cheap rent. And many of us live here, even though it's illegal. I'm certain the owner of the Grant knows this. Sort of a "Don't ask, don't tell" rental agreement.

Havana's been partying with friends, assures me she's not

returning Dennis's many calls, it really is over and she's moving in with Troy. She spots Ron Rosenbaum's book on my desk. "I did some E with Troy last night, and we watched this documentary on Hitler at like three in the morning. Troy said there's Hitler stuff on all the time in the wee hours."

I look at her through the veil of smoke off my cigarette. "He's right. After five hundred cable channels arrived, Hitler got a new lease on life."

She bums a cigarette, lights up. "This show was really cool. All black-and-white with captions. There was this huge rally. Thousands of people with all these torchlights and everybody holding up flags. The swastika you always get so excited about was *everywhere.* All these guys in black uniforms on old motorcycles riding in a parade. On E it's great. The thing must have been two hours long. Lot of it was Hitler waving his arms and speaking to the crowd. I didn't pay too much attention to the captions. He's screaming in German, and even though I couldn't understand it, I felt he made me higher than the E."

"Was the name of it *Triumph of the Will?*"

Her cigarette freezes, smoldering between her fingers, like one of those magnificent ruptures in Flagstone Walker's *Who is Thomas Jefferson?*

"Just a sec," she says, punching in a number on her cell. She talks to Troy. He confirms Leni Riefenstahl's notorious propaganda film of the 1934 Nuremberg party rally is still on. I must admit her film of torchlit rallies, demented pageantry and the demonical precision of troops marching toward a "New Germany" does create an oceanic effect that sweeps the viewer into the heart of the Third Reich.

I give Havana the lowdown on Riefenstahl's spectacle. Her take is different. "You're the one always yakking about the importance of history. Well, Hitler made a big dent in history, he was a trendsetter. I can't really hate on him. Really, I kinda like his evilness. He knew what he wanted and went for it."

"Gassing millions?"

"No, that's way wrong. Hey, Troy's a Jew. I mean more like, well, it was a trip to watch, like a light show on acid. Will you drive me over to Berkeley? I'll pay you ten bucks."

"Let's go."

Pulling up in front of Troy's house she says the public sex show at the Power Exchange gave her an idea. "Let's you and I do that, private shows in hotels. Advertise it as a young girl and an old guy, but not the uncle thing."

I smile greedily. "I'll run an ad in the next *SF Weekly*."

FOURTEEN

A bright blue morning in North Beach, warm biscuits at Café DeLucchi, a *Chronicle* headline: WHITE SLAVERY. What more could a pimp ask over coffee?

I'm not so cold-blooded that I lack any compassion for the "500,000 women trapped in a modern day slave ring" in Germany as the *Chron* announces. I don't doubt the Russian criminals who operate the "dreary Hamburg brothel" force some women to screw at least "ten customers per shift," or that one of the Russky pimps uses "a stopwatch to make sure the women are meeting their quota" and they get the crap beaten out of them if they don't. Ever since the collapse of communism in 1989, women from the Ex-Union of Soviet Socialist Republics and the former Eastern Bloc states have been brought into Western Europe with fake documents and promises of work as "hostesses" in nightclubs.

But I can't go along with the *Chron*'s assumption that half a million white girls are subjected to this kind of abuse. Enslaved-women stories always take a few worst-case scenarios straight from the mouths of the police and extrapolate them over all the women in the "cargo."

I'll extrapolate the other way. A Russian girl who spent a couple of months in Zen hooked her way into Germany, came to the United States on a temporary visa and, as far as I know, is still here. (If the women were pretty enough, Zen did not require green cards for employment.) One night, I asked Anastasia about the white-slavery stories. She had not been beaten nor abused. After paying a one-time fee to a pimp/smuggler to get out of Moscow, she was on her own. I asked Anastasia what drove her to this extreme, and got a one-word answer: "Freedom."

Though lucky enough to be young when the Iron Curtain melted in the flames of emancipation, she soon became aware that the power shift in the new Russia forced many well-trained docile servants of the bloated bureaucracy to comply with the demands of a far-ranging criminal enterprise along the lines of the Mafia.

The new state of affairs, only marginally better than the old, did provide Anastasia with something her parents never had: hope. Anastasia would not have been able to get out of the country under the old state apparatus filled with spies, informers, re-education committees, and collectivized kindergartens. Ruthless state power provides slaughter; ruthless capitalist criminals provide a measure of hope. Crime on a grand scale is a necessary stage on the road from communism to capitalism. She simply didn't want to wait it out.

The Russian Mafia is willing to sell "passports" at a price. The shrewd thugs are reaping the spoils from a great fire sale—the whole fucking state apparatus. The Mafia inserts itself in the middle of this merry-go-round, skims a piece off the top, or, in the case of prostitution, gets the lion's share.

The Reds have always claimed prostitution is a social evil produced by capitalism. The big daddy of dialectical materialism, Karl Marx, put it this way: "Money is the pimp . . . I am ugly but I can buy the most beautiful women."

Go, Karl.

Actually, the Daughters of Joy will flourish under any system. The decisive factor is how hard you want to crack down. Under a democratic system, hyping White Slavery stories helps a bit. The more victims, the better, so the public knows the depths of the disgraceful practice.

According to the *Chronicle*, about half the imported white slaves are in Germany, half in other Western European countries. Erring on the side of caution, assume the 250,000 German slaves fuck four men a day, failing to meet their quota of ten. Thus, a turnover of a million johns a day. How often does Sigfreid Wagner visit a brothel or pick up a girl leaning on the remains of the Berlin Wall? Assume *all* the Sigfreid Wagners need their clarinets polished once a month. Total tricks turned per month: thirty million.

According to a 1995 census, the male population over the age of fifteen in Germany is thirty million. So, if every man in Germany and some teenagers in need of training visit a brothel once a month, we could buy in to the quarter-mill number. Rather unlikely that German boys have that much stamina, despite their history.

A large hand appears over the plate on my table, a biscuit snatched away. I look up and see Richard May stuffing the whole thing in his mouth. "Good," he says, sitting down across from me.

"Jam?" I ask, pointing to the finger bowl of strawberry preserves.

"No thank you," he replies with exaggerated politeness.

I push the *Chronicle* toward him, point to another story, the Big Block gang's turf battle with Westmob in Hunters Point. A dozen or so guys have been killed in the gang rivalry that's been going on for a couple of years. "The guy who runs Big Block has a hip-hop record label called Big Block. I was thinking about calling him to see if I could score an interview. Seems like these hip-hop labels are always intertwined with gang connections. Think that's true?"

He reads a bit of the story. "Probably. If you tell the guy you're a pimp and the escorts get five hundred an hour, he'd be more willing to talk to you. He'll get a big surprise when your white face shows up."

"Maybe I'll go that route. Would give me credibility."

"Cred," Richard corrects.

"Right. And props."

Richard drops the newspaper on the table. "I gotta laugh when I hear people in San Francisco talk about how bad the gang problem is. Big Block! Westmob! Buncha clowns compared to the South Bronx. Remember that movie *Fort Apache*? I grew up two blocks from there. You should see the Savage Skulls. Now, there's a gang. These guys would line up ten deep and march down the street like this."

Richard lifts his 6'2" 200-pound frame out of the chair, wobbles mechanically like a goose-stepping Soviet.

"Did you put in an application for Savage Skulls?"

Richard sits down. "I was going to leave you the last biscuit," he says, taking a bite out of it. "I was screwed up, and Savage Skulls had some attraction. But even then I knew it was a dead end. There's one way to avoid the gang and still retain respect: Be a jock. I was a star on Playground No. 52."

His eyes shine brighter than I've ever seen. He glances out the window, the glory days in the South Bronx sweeping over him. He pulls a pencil from inside his jacket, leans over the table and starts drawing the first lines of a blueprint on a napkin.

"Huge. Playground No. 52 seemed to run as far as the eye could see. No grass. All cement for two full square blocks."

He draws a basketball court on the napkin. To get the full effect, he butts two more napkins up against it. He pauses, chews on the end of his pencil meditatively, begins filling in the outer napkin. "Over here, there's a baseball diamond. The lines were pretty well worn. But we could sight a line for right field from the catcher's mound out to a church steeple across the block," he says quietly, as the playground continues to fly off his pencil tip. "A water tower on the other side marked off left field. Not quite like Fenway Park, so lots of arguments on whether a ball was foul."

I try to imagine Richard's neighborhood years ago. Loud music, the sound of guns shooting up the 'hood, cop car sirens in the distance, pimps yelling at ho's on the corner, the pounding of boots burning through the night. Against these thunderous waves of indignation and cruelty, silence surrounds a shadowy figure on a concrete playground. Richard puts the pencil back in his pocket. "The church was about four hundred feet away. I never actually saw anyone pop one in there, but I heard it happened."

We leave the café, stroll through the crowded streets, past restaurants where the aroma pleasantly shifts from Italian to Chinese to Indian. A girl leans over the rail on the open terrace at Enrico's, kisses a man and runs off. The café habitues, shuffling through the morning papers, fill up the tables at Puccini's, Greco's, the Roma. At Caffe Trieste, the oldest coffeehouse in North Beach, many of the patrons are codgers, some OBs (original beatniks), some happily remaining comfortable in familiar surroundings, some brilliantly adrift, some alcoholics, some with bitter tongues.

Down the block from Caffe Trieste, the sound of bells signals a cloud to move on. Sunlight breaks through over the twin spires of St. Peter & Paul. And two men getting older move on, Richard and me, both of us still clinging to the dream that permeates every street and alley in North Beach: the dream of leaving a small mark among the poets, painters, and jazz musicians whose spirits float about us. Their spirits remain not only in books, on walls and records, but in the wind, the sunshine, and the fog.

• • •

Richard May clamps a spotlight on an I-beam, pulls out his latest from behind a stash, props it on a chair under the light. The reversed swastika on the canvas is so submerged you almost have to look for it. Really, several layered swastikas conveyed in such a way that it would be hard to accuse Richard of painting one at all. A real eye-swallower. Clean boundaries in metallic stoplight-green pigment.

I gaze at it for a while, and come to see it's not a swastika at all, but a near-perfect form.

FIFTEEN

avana calls with exciting news: The *SF Weekly* hit the streets yes-
terday, and she's been fielding calls for the new ad:

Relax & Watch

a

PRIVATE LIVE EROTIC

performance art show

by

KEN & KIA

Kia, a.k.a. Havana, has told callers the "performance art show"
examines the psychological dynamics of a sexual encounter between
an old guy and a young Asian/Latina/white mixed-race girl. She's
set up an appointment for 10 P.M. with a couple from Miami who
used to swing, have not swung for about ten years, but are thinking
about jumping back into the free-for-all. Kia's made it clear to all

who have called that the sexual doings will be restricted to the per-
formers onstage, though she's allowed that she would discuss the
ramifications of audience involvement in the play after we arrived at
the spectators' private theater.

I'm nervous as we go up the elevator at the Nikko, a hotel with
a cool luminous lobby, slick marble interior, and a highly overrated
sushi bar. To my surprise, the door at the end of the hallway opens
on an attractive couple. Damien and Leslie are both puffing away.
Within a few minutes, the room is nicely gray as we all make our
way through cigarettes. Havana—oops, I mean Kia—pulls out a
bottle of Merlot and a corkscrew from her bag, places them on a
table beside the bed. Leslie picks up the corkscrew. "You guys come
prepared!"

She hands the corkscrew to me, corrals two more glasses out of
the bathroom. I open the wine and pour out four glasses, pleased
that I'm not trembling in the least.

Leslie and Kia hit it off right away, due to a mutual interest in
tarot and astrology that allow properly schooled messengers like
themselves to tug the stars down to earth, comprehend the larger
patterns swirling through the energy fields of the Whole, and then
intertwine the data accrued from such investigations to insure the
mark's personal growth. Damien fills me in on reinforced concrete—as opposed to filling me *with* it, though I'm not sure the
latter wouldn't be preferable.

They tell us about the push/pull of swinging. The unceasing
entrances and exits at many ports of call had fulfilled their needs for

diversion, yet frequently had them closing in on divorce. Two kids, now nine and eleven, kept them together. "They are the air we breathe," says Damien. "No way we were going to split, even though Leslie is impossible to live with."

"That's true," admits Leslie as she puts her arms around him. "Damien thinks air is going to be bottled and sold pretty soon. He's an environmentalist, which I think is great, seeing as he runs a concrete company."

Kia sets down her wineglass. "That's cool. Everybody should recycle, and there's nothing wrong with cement."

I can't resist joining in. "We see nature ruling every time grass bursts through pavement."

Damien winks. "Not my pavement."

They tell us a few more swinging tales. Leslie points out that they now feel their bond of matrimony is secure enough to possibly re-enter the mountings and thrusting of the sex circus. "We figured it would be better to ease into it. When we saw your ad, it was like hey, this is purr-fect!"

Time for eye candy and an aging rake to get it on.

We begin with lots of kissing, slowly peeling each other's clothes off, slide into a creative body-licking interlude with my Rips on, her hard shiny butt rippling under a neon green thong. Damien and Leslie sit in chairs by the side of the bed, smoking, holding hands. I steer Kia around so they can focus on the flow of her aura radiating off those dancer's legs and flat tummy.

Act I blends seamlessly into Act II. Kia goes down on me for a long time. I contain her remarkable deep slides with several elegant withdrawals to prevent ending the show with an ill-timed climax. On Kia's fifth or sixth dive down, Leslie suddenly yells out, "Stop!"

I had heard them whispering to each other during the second act, so I worry that we're about to receive the Butcher of Broadway treatment. Or perhaps they want us to hasten to the next act. Or maybe they have another play in mind.

Finally Kia asks, "Are we doing something wrong?"

"No, no, no," Leslie assures us, "you guys are just beautiful together. It looks like you're really into it, and not at all phony."

This comes as a great relief to me. Like Flagstone Walker, I abhor bells and whistles tacked onto any artistic endeavor. All of my creative output is grounded in authenticity.

Despite the four-star review, we're told they simply can't handle any more erotic floods punishing the fragile dam of monogamy they've spent so long shoring up. Seems K&K's performance art has convinced them they do not want to return to Miami and go on a vile spree. Any possibility of returning to swinging is out of the question, especially since they'd made a decision some years back that their children would not be doing the visitation square-dance, or adjusting to stepparents.

We all hug, then K&K spring out of the Nikko into the street. I hand the $300 fee to Havana, drive her to Berkeley to see Troy, who knows what we're up to and has no problem with it. Havana's ecstatic over our life-affirming act that has saved a marriage. She believes more K&K theatrical productions could bring peace to the world; the United Nations can soon declare itself out of business.

I'm pretty ecstatic myself as I glide back over the bridge. On Market, traffic is light at this hour. During the day, it's jammed with cars, SUVs, buses, trolleys, trucks, and the brave on bicycles. The diagonal lance causes monstro traffic jams, but I don't care. All those V intersections with triangular buildings are the perfect symbol for a city always on tilt.

I make a right on Sixth, slow down in front of cherry bars flashing and crinkling atop two cop cars blocking the street, a third angled over the curb, one front wheel on the sidewalk. I stop, roll down the window. A cop stretches his steel arms across the block while four others decorated with nightsticks, keychains, guns, and cell phones mill around two guys being handcuffed. A flashlight shines into a spooky face, an interrogating finger explores the perp's mouth, digging out a balloon of crack from behind the gums. The head is pushed down, and the dude tumbles into the backseat of a squad car.

A flashlight beam slants across the sidewalk, bends up the wall, lands on another face. The guy turns and runs, gets about five feet before he's grabbed. Then the idiot swings on the cop, landing a punch to the jaw. Blue uniforms pounce all over him, take him down to the pavement. He continues to flail and struggle. Blue fists pummel away. They finally stand him up, his face covered with blood.

I hear a hard steely tang in a cop's voice. "Keep moving." I ease my way around the bust, swing back up the block, and pull into the alley behind the Grant Building. Down the alley, a wine-drenched rag picker on top of a Dumpster fishes around, pulls out a hat and tries it on. Hat in hand, he climbs off the Dumpster. In the pale silence of blackness, God or Satan as my witness, he takes a shit in the hat.

After completing a fouler worthy of a poem, he carefully tosses the hat back in the Dumpster. Oh, how a song of San Francisco can thunder in the heart of the night! Too bad Supervisor Gavin Newsom wasn't on hand to witness it.

The alley between the Grant and the Court of Appeals is a vast open urinal. The city tried to ease the problem by installing more public toilets, but that only complicated matters, since the toilets have become a comfortable place to shoot up heroin. Or, as Newsom put it, they are a haven for "uses not necessarily in line with our original concept."

I walk quickly up the alley, needing to get into the Grant before my bladder bursts. Instead, I do something I've never done before: whip it out and piss on the side of the building. With the free spirit coming out in me, I decide not to go back to my office and write, but rather pursue something "not necessarily in line with my original concept."

I get back in the gold pile, cruise around town under the neon glow spreading across the sidewalks in sheets of sparkling pink, yellow, and blue. Headlights loop and bend, spraying long white rays into the city of night. I thread through a dark canyon of hotels, shoot up Russian Hill, turn right at the top, drive slowly along California, pass the Fairmont, the Huntington, the Mark Hopkins, Zen's favorites. Crossing Powell I look at the lights glimmering in skyscrapers that continue to shoot up higher and higher, banging against the stars.

I love this night, a night when the inner world merges with the outer one. I can feel the city in my blood. San Francisco, the mistress of America! A gray city of mist and fog, a cool city battered by strong winds, a magic city waving its wand over little steel boxes jerking and rattling up Hyde on a cable of wire. The smell of Peet's coffee in the morning, the fragrant aroma of pork and bok choy in Chinatown in the afternoon, the sound of music in the streets of SOMA on Saturday night, the church bells ringing over the Mission on Sunday morning.

A city of seekers.

At this hour in the morning, my hands gripping hard on the steering wheel as the gold pile screeches in a series of circles winding up to Coit Tower, I revel in doing my part to keep salaciousness alive and well in this bastion of lust. I park, saunter over to the edge of Telegraph Hill and look out at Alcatraz winking at me. Black waves roll out of the Pacific. The moon is full, throwing down streaks of white light rippling across the dark waters sliding under the Golden Gate. Lights twinkle off the Bay Bridge, and beyond, the soft hills of the East Bay sleep under the sky.

I twirl back down the hill, out into North Beach, back up Russian Hill, driving fast, the gold pile dipping and bobbing along streets paved over steep ravines and jutting hills, past old Victorians tossed against the earth, condos hanging precariously from cliff edges. As I race over the top of the highest hill, a mighty wind swoops under the wheels, and I'm carried up into the night sky on a whirlwind and find myself in a gold chariot pulled along by a team of four red horses.

I lean over the edge, hear the bells of St. Francis of Assisi and Old St. Mary's, as the red horses race along in wide concentric circles spiraling upward. Seven square miles of bright light begin to shrink and fade into white dots. I feel light as a butterfly, standing in my gold chariot, whip in hand. I raise it, slash down on the horses' flanks. "Go Cordelia, go Shannon, go Saigon, go Havana—up, up, up!"

Snorting furiously, my stable carries me higher. We sail past the face of the moon, out into the blackest of black, into the stars, my red horses throwing a rosy silver light off their manes. Flames flare forth from a thousand suns. Banking across a black hole outside of time, zigzagging through the Milky Way, I pick up a red spear and toss it across a comet's tail.

Tumbling through infinity, my red horses rear up in front of an exploding star. We do a loop-de-loop and begin plunging back, down a long arc of time. We flip forward again, race ahead, and I give a thumbs-up sign to tiny Pluto still struggling in search of his orbit. Just as my gold chariot swerves under Saturn's outer ring, I get a call on my cell. *NORMAN, wondering when I'd hear from you . . . Oh, that's great, must have been a relief to spend some time in New York and get out of this stinkhole . . .*

My red horses surge ahead on their own, sparkles of light flash beneath their grinding hooves. I toss the whip into space, sit back against a velvet pillow. Panting, sweating and heaving, they tear past Mars and gallop back into the winds above the Golden Gate, ease down on top of the hill and lightly trot, trot, trot on high heels back to the stable, while I brush the comet dust off my jacket. The gold pile coasts down the hill.

SIXTEEN

Flagstone Walker's in motion again, this time on location at the Europa, a rundown hotel in the heart of North Beach. His scheming, art-damaged mind has conjured up another Dogma 95 political porn film: *Who Is Fidel Castro?*

Havana stars under the name Havana Castro; in fact, she's the only person in the film. He regards this work in progress as a "monologue of splendor against the summary judgment of Fidel's naked power." He intends to use that cheesy Compare & Contrast as a cutline under a naked black-and-white photo of Havana in his PR release.

To his credit, he is abstaining from speed during this production (rarely can Flagstone be given credit for anything, other than a certified membership among San Francisco's 50,000 bad artists churning out stupefying crap). The last time out, he was so baked on meth, he erased the entire film by taping over it when he turned his camcorder on a graffiti artist perched on the fire escape, spraying a huge blob on the side of the Odd Fellows Hall.

He's been drinking heavily at the Europa for three days, including a marathon wine binge with Havana at the Fuse on Broadway the previous night, where his fragile ego received a lift: Havana introduced him to the bartender, who immediately recognized his alter ego's byline. "Those stories you write for the *Chronicle* are the best thing in the paper."

"Thanks," he'd replied calmly, while his heart skipped deliriously, and he told himself if this esteemed reader happened to be gay, he'd be willing to blast through to the other side for the first time in his life. Give this man a blow job!

The corner room in the Europa overlooks the intersection of Columbus and Broadway, perfect for Havana, who wants to do one scene dancing naked in front of the window. Flagstone has spent two days holed up, drinking and writing the script on a yellow legal pad. He believes writing the script on location will give *Who Is Fidel Castro?* greater authenticity.

Or some, anyway.

Two additional factors led to this location: first, the Europa occupies the two floors directly above the Condor Club, now a beer-and-pool joint, but best remembered as home to Carol Doda, the white-booted go-go dancer whose hefty siliconed tits went topless in 1964. A white piano anchored to a steel pole would drop down from the ceiling with Carol strutting her stuff atop it. The descending white piano gimmick continued long after Carol left the Condor Club, by way of a splendid *deus ex machina* one night in 1983: After the patrons had been cleared out and the doors locked, the bouncer invited his favorite topless dancer to fuck on top of the famous piano.

In the midst of their fornication, the hydraulic mechanism jammed, sending the piano on its upward slide. A fatal erotic ascent, the bouncer crushed to death between piano and ceiling. The couple lay pinned together until the janitorial crew arrived the next morning. Nasty cleanup. The dancer survived, but soon left San Francisco, never to return.

Second, Flagstone wants to film in a hotel room that hearkens back to Castro's New York moment in 1960. Having come to power the year before, Fidel made his triumphal visit to the UN even more thrilling when President Eisenhower foolishly refused to invite him to lunch at the Waldorf-Astoria on Park Avenue. Castro played the snub beautifully: he checked into a Harlem dive, Hotel Teresa, saying he would be "honored to lunch with the poor and humble people of Harlem."

Flagstone envisions the white piano and the Europa's ratty interior as visual twin tropes, if you will, similar to the interpolation of a jarring phrase in the authorized service of the medieval church. The cultural elite Flagstone yearns after will easily pick up on the hotel trope, but he's struggling to find the right aesthetic trajectory that will allow him to incorporate a representation of the bloodied white piano.

At this hour, Flagstone's elated by a lucky break: perhaps a third trope that will advance his cinematic storyline. Returning from a liquid lunch at Vesuvio's, he finds a letter shoved under the door. He picks it up, catches the strong smell of perfume, turns it over and sees in small handwriting: "Dan, Room 213."

Must be for the previous occupant. "Tough shit, Dan," mumbles Flagstone, wondering what words lie hidden under the perfume. He opens it, finds a girl struggling with English as a second language:

Dear Dan:

Hi there!

How have you been doing lately? If you can't remember me, please forget below sentences.

I'm very fine except for one thing. It's you, Dan. I know my friends and you think I'm silly. I think so, too, because I already have boyfriend. But I might lose my mind because I miss you so much.

Did you make a phone call? Did you miss me? Do you still want to keep me? I want you to keep in touch.

And can I trust you? You said that you never leave me. I think I can. I don't know if you still want me to keep or you've just got a new girlfriend.

Please call me. I'll be home. Bye!

Love,

Kim

P.S. If you care, just throw away this letter. I'll be fine. But

I want you to know I'm always thinking about that night,
I was in your room with you.

Kim's phone number is at the bottom. Flagstone's tempted to call her, see if she might want to be in the film, then decides his mail intrusion might only irritate her.

Havana returns from the beauty parlor like a butterfly emerging from a cocoon, blonde with a streak of blue blazing in the afternoon light, long blonde hair falling and unfurling over her shoulders, soft curls tickling the sides of her neck, blonde and streaked like Bianca's without a trace of that skanky bitch's personality.

Flagstone gazes at her smooth skin, straight nose, finely curved cheeks, lips damp and glistening. She smells of soap and perfume. Flashing out of the blondeness, those velvet-black eyes are so big they seem to fill half her face. Brown stiletto shoes, low-rise tan cigarette-slim pants skimming up her stylized bod, a high-cut light yellow baby T.

She loves those Ts, has them on her closet shelf stacked to match all the colors in the rainbow. Yet each time out for a new tiny T is an agonizing experience. She has complained on many occasions that she is forced to shop in the children's department for tops. Women's wear seldom stocks a size one for her teeny-bopper slim frame. Poor beautiful Havana, the trials and tribulations she must endure, spiraling up the escalator to Nordstrom, searching in vain for a size one, compelled to shop amongst the kiddies with lollipops. Be advised when she issues this protest it pours from her mouth with heavy emphasis on size *one.*

The size-one blonde bats her eyelashes. "The new me."

Flagstone picks up the camcorder. "You look fantastic. Ready for the shoot?"

Havana picks up the script, swings her arm in a half-circle through the air. "Sure, I got it all memorized. Sorta. Are you sure we got enough candles?"

"I bought fifty, but we probably won't need them."

Havana runs her hand along the stepladder she painted green and yellow for the production. "Since there are four steps, I was thinking it might be good to paint two of them red."

Flagstone shakes his head. "It looks great the way it is. Let's crank this baby off. Walk slowly toward the bed as you say the first four lines."

He sets the camcorder on the tripod. What he has in mind is the esteemed contemplation of a Dogma 95 work of art merged with MTV's style of instant gratification through mindless fast cuts. He begins with a close-up of her hand while panning the camera back. Havana holds up a pack of Export A's. "These are Canadian cigarettes. My mother is white. My father is Cuban. The blood of the mall rats in California and the Cuban masses runs through me."

She flops down on the bed on her back with her head hanging over the edge, takes out a cigarette and lights it. "When I smoke Canadian cigarettes, I feel like totally . . . internationalista."

Flagstone shoots a close-up of her lips exhaling a thick line of smoke, then, for a smoking fetish dollop, the tip of the cigarette as she deeply inhales another drag. She speaks in a low tone. "Look how my Canadian cigarette flickers with aesthetic importance."

Flagstone stops shooting. "Perfect. Let's do the strip routine."

Havana slips Troy's drum and bass CD in the tray, turns up the volume. Flagstone shoots her strip show, turning the camera on and off in five-second segments. Havana tosses off her shoes, peels off her pants, prances about in a red thong and the yellow baby T. After about a minute, Flagstone slowly turns down the volume on Troy's mutilated music as Havana steps back and sits on the window ledge, her hands cupped over a raised knee. "I am *not* related to Fidel Castro. He is an asshole. In 1968, Castro nationalized sixty thousand small businesses like snack vendors and bicycle repair shops, saying the owners were 'bloodsuckers conducting their commerce in the shadows.' The result—"

Flagstone cuts in. "Wait, you forgot to do the finger quotes starting with 'bloodsuckers.'"

Havana sticks her finger in her mouth and makes a heaving sound. "I had a teacher who did that all the time. Just so picky-picky about everything, especially homework. God, his fingers were always doing that dance, like that meant . . . this is really *important*. A wuss. People who do finger quotes are stupid."

Flagstone rapidly shakes his head left and right, fingers slashing repeated quotes in the air. "You're regressing with the stupid thing again. I'm the director, so *quoth* with your fingers."

Havana raises her middle finger in the air. "Can I do this after the finger quotes?"

Flagstone punches his fist in the air. "Brilliant. A perfect follow-up to Fidel saying 'bloodsuckers conducting their business in the shadows.'"

Take 2 proceeds. After Havana flips the bird, she continues: "Castro's policy sent the economy into the tank, so in 1995 he allowed the bloodsucking snack vendors back into business. On top of that, he begged global corporations to invest in Cuban agriculture and industry. One country in particular."

She pauses, once again holds up the pack of Export A's. "Canada."

Cut. Havana sits on the ladder, strokes the creamy surface of her thigh below her thong. Shoot. "My last boyfriend was from Canada. He was nice, but this one thing he wanted from me I could never do."

Cut. She steps off the ladder, moves behind it, puts her head between the top two steps, her blonde hair nicely backlit with the sun filtered through the dirty window. Shoot. "When we made love, he always wanted me to talk dirty to him. I don't know why, I just can't do that."

Cut. She gets on her hands and knees, and puts her head between the two lower steps. Shoot. "There's nothing wrong with dirty talk, but for me"—she twists her neck upward—"it's a ladder I just can't climb."

Flagstone's mad hand picks up the scrawled script, waves it in her face. "*Ambition's* ladder."

Havana crawls out from behind the ladder, stands up, grabs the script out of his hand. "I know you want it hokey, but that's *so* lame. Nobody—"

"Not hokey. Post-mod camp," Flagstone interrupts.

"Whatever. Nobody would say 'ambition's ladder.'"

"How about *Shakespeare*? 'Lowliness is young ambition's ladder.'"

She snaps back. "You're the one yapping about context all the time. Like a girl in a thong would *really* say something like that?"

Flagstone laughs. "Yeah, okay, like the hip-hoppers say, we gotta 'keep it real.' Okay, let's move on." Havana sits cross-legged at the foot of the stepladder. She looks straight into the camera and, as directed, breaks the Fourth Wall: "So I left my boyfriend, and now I want to be with you. Only you. Let's climb the stairway to heaven arm in arm, just the two of us." She gets up, climbs up the ladder, reaches her inviting arm out to any and all only-you's, sits down on the top step. "You are such a cool guy, I *will* try talking dirty to you."

Havana bounces off the ladder, gets down on all fours, then crawls forward, lowers her voice. "Do you like it when I crawl on my hands and knees toward your (beat) big hard (beat) Being? I want to suck your Being."

Flagstone turns off the camcorder. "This is great. You really know how to vamp it."

"Easy to do with lines like that," she yowls. "I better get going. Maybe I'll ask the john if he wants me to suck his Being."

"Do that. Let me know his reaction."

The sun-haired girl checks herself out in the cracked mirror above the stained sink, takes off for Zen duty. Flagstone floods his heart with more wine, fools around with what he claims is a script for a couple of hours until Havana blasts back in. "If you really want to do a movie, I got a real story for ya. This guy was way spun on speed. What you do is nothing compared to him. He must have snorted ten fat lines while I was there."

Flagstone pours wine in a paper cup, spilling it out over the top. He wipes the sides of the cup with a napkin, hands it to her. "If I did ten lines I'd never sleep again. And I'd spill wine all over the place."

Havana kicks off her shoes, sits on the edge of the bed. "That's okay. You can always get more wine."

She makes a toast, takes a sip. "This guy looked like a typical tourist down on Fisherman's Wharf. Wore a Hawaiian shirt and cut-offs. Had a hairy chest and a few of the buttons had popped off his shirt. Real nice, ordered Champagne which came with a big fruit bowl. The bellboy was a really cute white guy. The guy gave him a hundred-dollar tip, so I knew it was gonna be a big score for me. But I was surprised when he asked me if I wanted to fuck the bellboy. And the bellboy was *really* surprised."

Flagstone picks up the legal pad and scratches down some notes. "This is great shit."

Havana gets up and moves toward the window. "Will you shoot some footage of me dancing in front of the window?"

"Yes, but not now. Don't leave me hanging just when your story is hitting the high point."

Havana dances a bit in front of the window, turns around.

"Okay . . . I ask the bellboy for a glass of Champagne. He pours it out real professional-like, and hands it to me. I smile and hand him a condom. Then I get off the bed and lean over it. The bellboy fucked me doggy-style. It was good, but he came in about two minutes. The john loved it. All he wanted to do was watch. When the bellboy was buckling his pants and getting ready to leave, he said, 'I'll never forget this for the rest of my life.'"

Flagstone nods. "I'm sure he won't. That might make a good movie, but let's take them one movie at a time."

There's a thump on the wall and a girl screams. "They're at it again," says Flagstone. A smack dealer in the next room goes at it constantly with his girlfriend. He has a sign on his door worthy of his profession: "Day Sleeper." An old nutcase down the hall who whistles Beatles tunes over and over had told Flagstone the couple never fuck. According to him, the girl only stays with the dealer so she can get her fix. Flagstone had asked the nutcase what the dealer gets out of that. "Somebody to yell at," he'd replied.

A door slams next door. Flagstone goes out in the hall, sees the dealer storming down the stairwell. He goes back in the room, tells Havana the coast is clear for the next scene. She throws on a robe and they go down to the end of the hallway. She takes off the robe. Flagstone films her twitching butt parading naked back to the room. Just as she gets to the doorway, the nutcase appears. Havana scoots inside. The nutcase looks at Flagstone, sees her robe thrown over his shoulder and the camcorder in his hand. "Nice stuff. Making a porn movie?"

"No, just a home video for her mother."

The nutcase pulls his net worth out of his back pocket. "I got eighty bucks worth of food stamps. Sell 'em to you forty bucks."

"I'd do it, man, but I'm flat busted," Flagstone bullshits. "Try the manager."

The nutcase shrugs, walks away. Back in the room Havana's slipped into a short skirt and a familiar baby T. "That dude happy, getting a peek at my ass?"

Flagstone tosses the robe on the bed. "Made his day. Okay, let's do the next scene following the hallway."

Flagstone zooms the camera in for a close-up on her face. Havana throws off a sultry look. "Did you like the triumphant march of my beautiful body?"

Flagstone lifts the camcorder away from his face with an exaggerated dramatic gesture. "Excellent. You're so good at doing these scenes in one take. Now comb your hair in the mirror while I shoot over your shoulder."

Havana twists up her face. "It's dirty, and it's got a big crack in it."

"That's better. Heavy symbolism with cracked mirrors."

She waves her comb over her head. "*You're* cracked." She picks up the script, mumbles the next few lines. Flagstone moves behind her, turns the camcorder on. She begins combing her hair. "I walked out on that Canadian dude while he was on the chatline getting some dirty talk from some ugly bitch. The chatline cost fifty cents a minute, and he spends over $400 a month on it."

Next up on his thong-ripping Dogmatist agenda, Havana plops

down on the bed and pulls out her nail polish. A close-up shot of her painting her right toe, slow pan back while Havana looks at her toe and queries: "Why did Fidel Castro become a dialectical materialist? How can the revolutionary fire still burn after jailing dissidents and fucking up Cuba for forty years?"

She continues in a voiceover while Flagstone has in the frame the image of a sign he'd printed out on his computer in large red Rockwell Extra Bold: "Hotel Teresa."

"I mean the history of communism is just one big mass grave filled with 85 million people since 1917."

Shot of graffiti Havana painted on the wall: "Fidel was here. 1960." Shot of masking tape holding some ceiling plaster in place. Return to toe painting.

"Why do men like Castro want to turn genocide into a system of government?" Shot of stained sink drain. "And why does my ex-Canadian boyfriend want to talk dirty on the phone?"

Shot of Havana switching the polish action to her left foot. "Is that the result of go-go capitalism causing alienation? Or does he like to hear dirty talk because he's stupid? Sometimes, I think my thoughts are too profound for my own good. So I cast away these thoughts and dance."

Flagstone blasts Troy's thumping CD with his left hand and keeps the camcorder on with his right, while Havana sets the toe polish on the bedside table, stands on the balls of her feet, twirls around, bends over and touches her toes, her skirt riding up her ass. The dance scene runs about thirty seconds, ending with Havana stripping off her top in front of the camcorder, then quickly spinning around and shaking her tits in front of the window.

Flagstone focuses in on a printed sign that reads: *Produced, directed, written, and filmed by Flagstone Walker.*

He then whirls around with the camcorder: Havana pulls a foot-long wooden match from a box, holds it in front of an Export A.

Flagstone begins zooming in on the match lighting the cig. We hear Havana's last words: "Oooh, look at the flame flickering with aesthetic importance."

Fin.

SEVENTEEN

'm panicking.

A girl who started working for Zen less than a week ago calls. She's furious, tells me she got busted at the motel where I dropped her off; the cops let her go, and I'm an asshole. "You should be able to smoke out the vice if you knew what you were doing."

I blast over to Richard May's apartment. The former pot dealer is convinced that I've been targeted, urges me to shut down Zen—if not permanently, at least for a few months. I agree. I cool it out for a few weeks, figure I'm not being targeted until two vice cops with ten-pound boots and a search warrant come smashing into my office in the Grant Building.

They cuff me. Zen's zapped.

The cops cart away thirty-nine items under the search warrant, including an eightball of speed, an ounce of pot, and two books: *Pimp* by Iceberg Slim and *Adolf Hitler and the German Trauma* by Robert Edwin Herzstein. (What gives? Do they think I'm a Nazi pimp?)

Now I'm sitting in the slammer, wondering why the hell the cops would bother with me. I wasn't doing the Iceberg Slim pimp/ho number on the stroll—*"Hey bitch, I don't care if it's pouring buckets, get yo bootie out there and walk between the raindrops"*—Zen only lasted about eight months, and I wasn't making tons of money that could be confiscated to fill the city coffers.

Still, I'm not being railroaded: just getting what I deserve. Christ, I'm a furburger broker, and I leave speed and pot right out in the open. I'm terrified, charged with one count of pimping and two counts of selling drugs. A *triple* felony.

I'm also terribly embarrassed and ashamed that in a city that properly recognizes and cultivates sodomy and the marvels of multicultural perversions, I get taken down for orchestrating the hopelessly simple pleasures offered by old-fashioned straight sex from an escort service.

What the fuck will the judge do to me? Might Judge Doom send me into a darkened pit where the great fear of all straight men behind bars will come to pass? Will it be one 200-pound candyman or a gang bang? Even worse than dropping the soap is replaying my stupidity over and over. Why didn't I hide the speed? Why did I have so much around? Well, I like having a good supply on hand, in case my dealer, who eats, snorts, and shoots gobs of meth, either disappears or ODs.

After the first twenty-four hours replaying the whole thing out, wallowing in my own pity, thinking about my life as a series of monumental failures, getting no sleep, I decide this is getting me nowhere and discover the second, third, and fourth days are carbon copies of the first. The initial terror finally recedes, but being locked up is complicated by another matter—no paper. No pens or pencils. I do find three books under a stack of toilet paper by the shower: A romance novel, *Kissinger* by Walter Isaacson, and *Checklist for the Perfect Bar Mitzvah.*

I have no idea how the books got there, but I now know more about Henry Kissinger than I did when he was conducting the nation's longest war. My favorite factoid is not on Richard Nixon's Machiavelli, but the American statesman, Henry Stimson, who, when asked why America should not set up a spy agency, replied, "Gentlemen do not read other people's mail."

Why can't vice cops with search warrants catch on to this?

As a general rule, I'll read whatever is around, but I draw the line at bodice-ripping potboilers, so I pass on the romance novel. With regard to the third tome, I would like to send out an emergency appeal to Jews: when I get out of jail, for a nominal fee I can help throw one dynamite Bar Mitzvah.

I've asked several guards—deputy sheriffs—for something to write with, and all have declined. Finally, one of them tosses me a pencil two inches long. I have one piece of paper—a duplicate copy of my "property record," an itemized list of my clothing taken when I was processed in. I take down a few notes in tiny handwriting on the property record and the inside back cover of the Bar Mitzvah paperback. This thrills me, pretending to be a prisoner, like Solzhenitsyn facing the annihilator in the Gulag.

. . .

My name is called, the cell opens, and I'm escorted to F-pod, one of five open circular dormitory-like facilities in the new section of the San Francisco County Jail. F-pod is about the same size and eeriness level as a crop circle. An elevated guard tower stands in the center of the two-level pod. This allows the deputies a full view of all inmates, about a hundred of us. We're in open four-man cubicles with bunk beds. No bars in F-pod. Just a steel door. I'm surrounded by dime-bag drug dealers, wife beaters, winos, and shoplifters. These guys are not Jeffrey Dahmer's lunch companions. The deputies call us "gentlemen." We're separated from the murderers, rapists, pedophile priests, and the like, who are housed in tighter quarters.

We move about freely most of the day. A chin-up bar and tread-mill for working out. A Ping-Pong table. Lots of chess games along with dominoes, checkers, and Monopoly. The food isn't great, but you can't expect sushi in the slammer. Lunch is the worst: usually a peanut butter sandwich on white bread with an apple. Outfitted in orange sweatsuits, we all look alike and spend most of the time walking around in circles like zombies.

We're also in various states of depression, some hovering on the pathological. Maggothead is the worst. He's around twenty-five, stocky, thinning brown hair, and has small brown eyes that see a disease-spreading conspiracy directed at all people behind bars. He's in the restroom with a rolled-up towel, awaiting the arrival of ferocious maggots assembled under the shower drain. From this submerged army an occasional maggot slips through, only to fall victim to the swatting of a vigilant orange towel. I haven't seen any maggots, but Maggothead assures me this is the case, and furthermore he will file a complaint with the *state* health department in order to override *city* health department officials who have cut a deal with the jailers to keep F-pod infested with an exotic assortment of bacteria.

A deputy escorts me into a small room where I see my lawyer, Bob Berg, whom I picked out of the phone directory purely because he does not run an advertisement for himself.

I've been in jail for a week, and he's not very encouraging. "You can put up bail money if you want, but the incarceration system looks a bit more favorably on those who wait right here while the wheel of justice is greased. Be patient."

Be patient? In here?

I've never tried heroin, but right now I'd like a buck-o shot of smack. Let that warm bath of China White wash over this pimp's bag of flesh. Send me down, down, down into the calm serene void where emptiness reigns and the only thing I want out of life is to float on an endless sea of dark waters.

Smack not available, my mind swings in the opposite direction. In jail, I'm struck by an obvious truth: *life has meaning*. For those who live on the edge, who concluded long ago we are but specks in some cosmic nonplan, the loss of freedom jettisons existential nausea, and life on the outside, with all its tortured angst, looks damn good indeed.

The day after I see my lawyer, a deputy approaches with his arm in the air, twirling a set of cuffs, and yells, "Bob Armstrong, come over here."

He hauls a bunch of chains out of a box, shackles me all over serial-killer style. We pass through the steel doors, out into the blazing sunlight. *Air, real air.* Feels so nice, for about two minutes. Head bent down, chains rattling, double-handcuffed, I'm shoved into the backseat of a patrol car. Off to San Francisco General Hospital, where a doctor will check me over and take a careful look at an "aberration" on an X-ray taken earlier at the jail's Med pod.

I see the Doc, go sit on a bench and wait. A cute nurse walks by. I miss my beautiful Zen dolls. All over, out of business, gone.

I wanna smoke, can't have one, and I'm turning over the aberration possibility. Ordinarily I'd be mortified, but now: three cheers for lung cancer! Mutate on! Surely the judge will only slap me with probation knowing death is near. What little money I've got left I'll spend in sushi bars stuffing myself with unagi and yellowtail while the Big C eats away at my lungs. I'll have time to get my affairs in order before facing infinity eyeball to eyeball.

Then I'll play my trump card: Vietnam. At last, those days in the rice paddies are going to pay off. The Cao Dai's big eye has finally blinked.

So glad I joined the Marine Corps! *Semper fuckin' Fi.* I'll hobble out to the Fort Miley VA hospital, coughing and hacking all the way, suckin' up those Camel Light Wides till the bitter end.

Maybe along with lung cancer I'll end up with a triple bypass and the prostate humdinger for good measure. Real nice view of

the Bay out at Fort Miley, like a sanitarium on the Magic Mountain. I'll sit in a red plastic chair with a shawl over my shoulders
and read books till the final cigarette casts me down into a river of
shit, Dante's eighth ring of Hell: *"Move on, you pimp, there are no women
here to sell."*

Not to be.

The Doc returns, tells me the aberration is nothing, but assures
me maggots and worms will be all over my X-ray if I don't stop
smoking. I'm reshackled and return to F-pod where Slicer and
Slinky are doubled over in laughter, right fists with thumbs and
forefingers curled in circles slashing through the air like piston
rings stroking along imaginary three-foot cocks protruding from
their orange crotches. This mock masturbatory exercise is directed
toward Queen Gene, who is in a cubicle on the opposite side of the
pod. The gay man has not been attacked, but Slicer, Slinky, and a
few other jerks subject Queen Gene to occasional verbal abuse and
limp-wristed gestures, though always at a distance.

Pistoning on, Slicer and Slinky mumble short staccato phrases
mixed with rap. "Yo, butt boy, watch out . . . backyard boogie . . .
suck-o, suck-o, suck-o, dough, dough, doughnut hole . . . five-shot
on Polk Street . . . Fagotstein . . . butt pirate, pre-pare to board . . .
Git the one-eyed trouser trout."

Both high school dropouts in their early twenties, they are high-
testosterone hets who strike me as gay nervous rather than gay
haters. For them, homosexuals are as remote as Martians, a strange
species beyond comprehension. However, in Slicer's case, they are

also an easy target, he tells me. When not behind bars, he hangs out on Polk Street, pretends to be a boy toy, gets picked up and agrees to give a blow job for thirty bucks. After getting the money, he pulls a knife: "I never cut 'em, I just take the thirty and disappear," he says with a shrug.

Slinky, 6' 4", rail-thin, runway model face, light black skin, hopes to score with rap when he gets out. All the young jailbirds slide around F-pod rapping. I notice Slinky is one of only a few who take the time and trouble to write down the vitriol. A ray of hope there. He's in for assault, made nastier when his steel-toed boot slammed into the side of his opponent who was flat on his back on the street.

I'm adjusting to F-pod. Paper and pens available from the commissary along with candy and snacks—Snickers, Hershey bars, Butterfingers, Tootsie Twins, Oreos, Cheetos, Moonpies, and best of all, Cup-O-Noodles that can be cooked in F-pod's microwave.

Orange sneakers, too, at $10.50, though I pass, since my Serious Tactical boots I bought at Stompers have proven to be a hit. Fashion is paramount everywhere these days, even in jail. With orange as everybody's permanent uniform, only two fashion statements are available: footwear and haircuts. My boots receive many compliments. Locked up, shoes are like flags for a country. They say who you are. Cool shoes, you are cool.

No haircut for me. The inmates buzz each other with two sets of shears. F-pod style leaves the top uncut with the sides skinned all around about two inches above the ear. Thus, the head looks like a clenched fist popping out of the neck, topped with a mushroom.

Something else makes life easier: two bookshelves filled with a lot of donated junk yield *Tender Is the Night* and *A Farewell to Arms.* Also *Romeo and Juliet,* a change of pace from the Classic Comics version I read in high school. Only behind bars would I crack Anthony Trollope's *The Vicar of Bullhampton* and Jane Austen's *Emma,* books not the least pernicious, a word both authors favor and appropriate for my crime of moral turpitude.

Another winner, *Propaganda and the American Revolution* by Philip Davidson, explores the role of ideas disseminated through pamphlets, broadsides, and newspapers in determining the outcome of the revolution. The book examines propaganda from both sides, including this stanza from a poem by Jonathan Odell in support of the Crown:

> **By George's fam'd shield,**
> **We will never yield,**
> **To the pimps or the**
> **Armies of Louis.**

Fan-fucking-tastic! Washington, Jefferson, and Madison pimped for the frogs.

I want out, but I must admit, this jail is ideal for writing. I do write on the outside, but many diversions during any 24/7, uh, reduce my output. Here, the words flow off sheets of paper that float to the floor around my bunk.

I'm not the only one reading and writing. Turns out, jail requires classes for those doing longer stretches. Classes in English for the Hispanics; a GED course for the dropouts, a huge wedge of F-pod's demographic pie; a computer class; even a silly art class to pass the time.

Therapy classes rule. I feel like a gambler with a dead man's hand in Dr. Kure's Safe Space sessions, but my recent love of speed cries out for attention. Dr. Kure has a wild head of hair, and his nose quivers like a rabbit's. A soft-spoken former alcoholic, he marches through the twelve steps with ease, prods me not to dwell on the past or the future, but concentrate on the present, which is "a joyful time."

You gotta be kidding, Dr. Kure. F-pod joyful? "You like to write, so write down all your resentments," he suggests.

"Hmm, can't really think of any off the top of my head," I reply.

I'm sitting in a circle next to Smackfiend, a thirty-seven-year-old carpenter who picked up the habit from his girlfriend. He turns to me and says, "You got no resentments, that's cool. I got one. Drugs should be legal, and I resent the fact they're not. When I get out of here, next train stop is Druggie Junction. Last night, I dreamed of a gumball machine dispensing gumballs of heroin, and I was scooping them up fast as they poured out."

A late arrival walks in. I groan. Maggothead. He apologizes for his tardiness and starts unloading about the intruders in the shower who are very aggressive at this hour. I say, "Those maggots are carrying the remains of Al Capone's syphilis from Alcatraz into this place."

Smackfiend laughs, adds: "I wish they'd carry some heroin in."

Dr. Kure throws us a frown, raises his forefinger across his lips. Maggothead, his mouth twitching, reiterates that the loathsome cankers are not giving any quarter. "Nobody in here cares about this but me. But everybody's health is at stake," he whines.

Dr. Kure commends him on his concern, then turns his attention back to Smackfiend, explains that the problem "is not the drugs, but the thought you can't get off drugs."

He always circles back to this point, which lines up perfectly with a belief shared by almost everybody in F-pod: Mind is all; the body is accessory baggage. This reminds me of my childhood days watching my grandmother make huge bright quilts from patches of cloth. Quilts swirling with color, like flowers in a meadow in May, pure as a painting by Van Gogh. She'd lay aside her needlework, make a pot of tea and read Mary Baker Eddy's *Science & Health* aloud, raise her head and look at me over her glasses. Off to the Christian Science church, a place I have not entered since I was nine. Yet I retain a certain fondness for the founder that rests on her loopy and lofty metaphysical zingers. "What is matter?" she asks. "Nothing," she replies.

Knock on wood till you drop, but it ain't there. All is mind.

Hard for my venomous brain to believe all this mind power will do any good, but what do I know? All dressed out in orange like everybody else and wondering if tomorrow's morning could be a year or two away. *I hate orange.*

Most of the inmates are friendly toward each other, though in addition to the gay man, another pariah, Stinky, takes a lot of heat

("P.U., his feet stink so bad he musta been stickin' it up his own ass-hole"). Brainiac also runs into difficulty, unable to grasp jail etiquette. Not cool to sit down at a table with four guys you've never talked to before, and ask, "Is this the gangster table?"

Brainiac pushes the envelope further during a filling-out-forms session. The counselor, standing before thirty of us slumped inattentively in plastic chairs in one of the classrooms, gently explains how to circle the right educational level. "Eight only if you completed grade school, twelve only if you graduated from high school."

Brainiac raises his hand. "The highest number is sixteen. I have a master's degree plus a year toward a doctorate. Should I write in nineteen?"

Cold stares, sneers, snickering, a low mumbled, "Dr. Fuckhole."

The counselor thanks Brainiac for bringing this bureaucratic oversight to his attention, notes the form will be corrected, then adds dryly, "Sixteen will be good enough for our purposes."

Later in a private conference I mention to Brainiac that some in here might think he's an IQ basher, and words he has used in casual conversation among the gangsters, like "plethora," "oxymoron," and "invidious," might, well, give offense.

We're about the same age, both of us circled sixteen, so he takes my point, saying, "I just don't want to pretend being other than what I am." We're seated across from each other. He looks over the top of his wire-rimmed glasses, reaches out and touches two fingers on my right hand, slams me with a hardball: "Anybody mention to you the polish on your manicure is badly cracking?"

I tell him safe so far, that I tried unsuccessfully to scrape off the remains of the shine in the shower, that the Zen dolls had insisted a good pimp always gets manicures and pedicures, that I thoroughly enjoy this salon fabulousness, and ask if he's heard any hostile rumors about my pinkies.

He shakes his head, asks if I've heard any rumors that he's a pedophile.

I haven't and tell him if that one gets floated past me, I'll say Brainiac is no short eyes, he's running a Ponzi scam. He laughs, says that's fine. I do think that's why he's doing time, but he's told me he was the fall guy on some sort of investment scheme involving bonds.

Brainiac does not clue me in on how I might be able to skim some cream off the bond market, nor do I pick up any crime lessons, as one might expect in jail. But Blade, a twenty-year-old Native American, does give me a great tip on how to make an alcoholic wonder drink: Pruno. He warns that if it's not properly distilled, it will make you go blind. Pruno is sort of a generic term for a wide variety of hooch, depending on what fruits and sugars are available where you are incarcerated.

Blade, who sleeps in the bunk above mine, goes into some detail beyond my grasp on orange juice versus orange rind. He favors the latter, a pile of peelings ground up with thirty sugar packets and warmed in hot water from the sink. "You put all of it in a plastic bag and squeeze the bag real tight so there's no air in it," he says, clenching his fists. "Let it ferment for three days. The bag blows up. Dump the pulp in a towel, strain it out and you got jailhouse juice."

Blade has done several stretches behind bars. His first stop was Juvy at age eleven for stealing a car and wrecking it in a high-speed chase. He says he was sent to Juvy about ten times, once for assault with a deadly weapon during a gang fight in the Tenderloin. "That was straight out of the movies. I was with my boy on Eddy and Hyde. This car stops, turns out its lights. I hear 'bang, bang, bang' and see the sparks in the open back window. I rolled on the ground and got behind a car, but my boy got smoked. They got out of the car and put two in his dome."

I hesitate, ask, "You mean it was an execution-style killing?"

Blade slams the palm of his hand on the side of his bunk. "Sure was."

"How old was your friend?"

"Fourteen." He gazes out into the pod for a moment, a long split second in time stepping back into the darkness. "I fired three shots as they ran back and jumped in the car. Didn't hit any of 'em. They took off. I yelled, I'm gonna split your wigs. But I never got the chance. Cop cars came screamin' up the street. Arrested me, and none of them ever got caught."

Blade says his public defender did a good job of punching holes in the case, and he only spent a month in Juvy on a reduced charge. But shortly after he turned eighteen, he got drunk at a Giants base-ball game, started a fight, and pulled a pistol. That created pandemonium in the stands. The cops arrested him in the fifth inning. Six months on that one.

The gang-banging has brought other close calls. "This guy mopped me [jumped him], stabbed me in the lung, took all my money. I was spittin' blood and gasping for air, had to walk two blocks to a pay phone and call an ambulance myself. Another time I got lumped with a padlock, tried to do a fat ass cut outta there, but got clobbered by this big Samoan. I'd just bought new white shoes and a white windbreaker, and they was all red with blood."

Blade says he wants to try and get his act together when he leaves F-pod. However, his first step does not bode well. "I don't carry a gun any more. I could get ten years just for havin' it. Only thing I pack with me now is a knife."

I drop off the chin-up bar, turn around, see this young black dude with a huge smile on his face approaching, and already know what's up, 'cause it's happened every day since I got here, sometimes two or three times a day. Word spreads quickly in jail, and the word is out on me.

Maybe it was Valentine Jones who told others about me, though I've asked around about the Smiley-wielding gangster from Oaktown, and nobody knows if he's still somewhere in the jail. In any case, this guy is another echo from Valentine.

"You a pimp? This is not real! A *white* pimp. An *old* white pimp. How ya do that?"

Nice not having to worry about a hostile reception from the brothers in jail, but weird, since I'm tired, foolish, and way out of their game. But the boys from Hunters Point got me bagged as a super O.G. (old gangster). "I'm not dealing with thirty-dollar tossups on Capp Street," I say, then tell him the price.

His eyes widen. "Five C-notes? Yo, they'z must be fine stuff."

Steeped in gangster culture and rap's blood-soaked narratives, he assumes I operate by those rules. Iceberg Slim's runner swivels lightly on his toes, kicks his foot in the air, and points at my feet. "Youse got cool boots for bustin' the bitch in the butt if she gets outta line, right?"

"No," I snap, "there's a better way." I fill the young ace in on Cordelia, tell him there's no way the flash-blasting Brit import would tolerate a boot in the butt. "Make sure she likes you. Treat her with respect. Show concern when she babbles on about her lame-o boyfriend." (The Zen dolls always managed to hook up with losers.)

He listens, then gets to the main reason why he wants to pimp. "You getting' lotsa pussy, arencha?"

I note that Iceberg Slim warned against this. (*Pimp* is *The Catcher in the Rye* in housing projects across America.) "Do not dip your stick in the pie. You do one of your girls, she'll lose respect for you. And if she gets busted, she'll take you down."

My brothers in orange do not come across as brutal, though that's why some of them are here. Instead I discover the young men of all colors are wimped-out whiners, constantly getting written up for petty infractions like cutting in the chow line, tossing Cheetos bags on the floor, yelling across the pod, taking the single copy of the *Chronicle* to their bunks, or using one of the eight phones without getting permission from a deputy. I feel like I'm in a fifth grade classroom.

Along with Ping Pong, F-pod should have Play-Doh and a Lego bucket. The restraint exercised by the deputies dealing with this caravan of assholes is stupendous. A mild dose of police brutality would probably improve matters.

An egregious write-up comes down. Deputy Olsen, always on top of the beat, calls us together in a pod meeting to ferret out the guy who removed from the wall a list of those scheduled for court appointments and medical calls. "Who took that list down?" Deputy Olsen commands. "Don't try to play me. Who did it? Step out now."

Nobody steps forward.

With fire in his throat, Olsen sends us his bill. "Okay, I'm writing up everybody in here."

Guys start grumbling and yelling "Deputy Hater." Suddenly a tall, dignified O.G. I'd come to know, Maurice Gross, steps forward. "I did it," he says.

"No, you didn't," barks Olsen. "Step back."

Gross's fifteen-year-old son had been shot to death in a gang-related dispute. The shooter got away. Seeking revenge, Gross tracked the shooter down, shot at him, and missed. As he was walking home with his pistol in his hand, the police arrested him. He ended up doing six months for assault with a deadly weapon.

I'm struck when I hear the words "I did it" from a man in an orange uniform willing to take the rap for the rest of us while he's still grieving the loss of his son. A rare moment of courage in F-pod.

We're not written up. Deputy Olsen reconsiders, takes away two hours of our "free time" (meaning we're restricted to bunks and denied the joys of walking around in circles like zombies).

When we start the walk again, I cruise around with Gross, tell him that was a gutsy move. He shrugs, says, "It's nothing, a write-up don't bother me none." We walk and talk for a long time. At one point, he stops, sticks his index finger under his chin, gives me a cocky look, and says, "Tell me, Vanilla Slim—"

I remember nothing after that. I'm blown away by my new moniker. I take it as a high honor, though I'm sure Gross is not handing me a five-inch brimmed Fedora and the keys to a sunroof El Dorado. No, I'm certain Gross has another image in mind—likely a tall, thin, white guy attempting to Watusi at the Peppermint Lounge.

My record is clean, but my fear is magnified when I find out my case has drawn a woman prosecutor and a woman judge. If that isn't retribution against a pimp, I don't know what is.

I'm convinced the assistant D.A. is the San Francisco chairperson for the progressive feminist organization, Against the Penis, and a devoted fan of Andrea Dworkin. Oh man, she'll build up her case with a pile of damning facts so high, Alcatraz will be reopened solely for the pimp in the pod. And the judge, Wonder Woman II, flying around the courtroom in a black cape given to her by Supreme Court Justice Antonin Scalia, will overrule every motion, plea, and objection from my long-faced lawyer. Then Wonder Woman II will smash down that gavel and send me off to the Rock.

Way wrong.

After nineteen days in jail, Berg works a plea bargain: The drug charges are dropped, I plead guilty to one felony count of pimping, get sentenced to three years probation and time served.

I should have known that in the hands of women, nothing can impede the triumph of justice. With exquisite Austenesque calmness and gravity, these women weighed the matter of a pimp venturing too far in drunken folly. Their delicacy of feeling combined with coolness of judgment, just as nature prompted, reminds me of my grandmother, my mom, my editor, all the women who have ever passed through my life, even the Zen dolls.

No matter how badly we screw up, the women go easy on us.

EIGHTEEN

I have always viewed prostitution as a victimless crime. Looking back on my own experience, I'm not so sure. Even at $500 an hour, screwing for money isn't something to celebrate. Somebody once said, "You choose your own road to Hell if that's where you want to go." But choices are not made on the basis of free will alone. When a woman solicits a man, it's likely the *last* choice she makes.

People say "he's prostituting himself" when the guy in the next cubicle sucks up to the boss. Yet all of us have kissed ass at some point along the line. It strikes me most forcibly that such groveling is not analogous to selling beaver to a meatball shooting his spoo.

We need not pretend we have two bodies, one for sale and the other for love. I witnessed daily the escorts' struggle to manage their two selves: one body a cocoon of privacy, genuine innocence, almost childlike pleasures; the other secret, manipulative, and venal. Too often, the secret life escaping into the night loomed large and overshadowed the other. The girls wrestled with this, pretending to send out living copies of themselves. This neat divide, however false, illuminates the paradox of sex work: selling sex, yet withholding emotion.

After getting passed around like an after-dinner mint, will this leave a spiritual wound that can never heal? Has the woman entered the city without hope, with no possibility of escape? For many, yes; for the sharper tarts who can see the danger signs, no. For one Zen doll, I'm not sure what will happen, but I'll be there.

Havana.

The day I got out of jail, I headed straight to Vesuvio's and got drunk. I sat at a table upstairs downing Pale India Ale, looked at the ghosts lined up in the windows of City Lights Books. They didn't look back.

I thought about how weary the Zen dolls must have been, going to the closet to pick out the clothes, painting their faces, taking refuge in their disguises. I thought about a deaf man who called once; typed in his questions to a special operator who relayed them without a hint of judgment ("Does she have big breasts?"). I thought about the paraplegic who saw Cordelia, and Fred who benefited from Havana's special sunlight therapy.

Crimes? Or are these women nurses of the spirit?

By the time I drank my sixth beer—or was it the seventh?—I'm not sure what I was thinking. Except this: the tender hearts in Zen brought me out of my gloomy solitude.

At this point, Dear Reader, you could consider this memoir a work of prostitution by a pimp attempting to sell a bill of goods, though I've tried to give an honest account of my midnight deeds and the lives of the women who entered Zen. And I feel gratified by writing out what I know to be true of myself. You might also expect an awakening, a transformation of character, a realization that I changed for the better as I came face to face with myself.

Alas, I have not.

I have struggled mightily with my demons and found that I like them—sex on the run, coffee, booze, cigarettes, speed (touch and go on that one), irresponsibility, and *The New Republic.*

I pack away the bad days with the good, knowing that wherever I step, the earth will likely be mined below my Serious Tactical boots. Once in a blue moon, when I'm in the depths of depression, I lie down on a quilt given to me in my age of innocence, and peruse Mary Baker Eddy's *Science & Health.* While I remain a nonbeliever, I still like an occasional dose of Ms. Eddy's medicine: *"All is Mind and its manifestation, from the rolling of worlds, into the most subtle ether, to a potato-patch. . . . Truth unfoldeth forever."*

I staggered out of Vesuvio's, walked through Chinatown past the lacquered storefronts filled with jade vases, gold jewelry, and bright trinkets; past an arcade draped with lame logo'd T-shirts, blue jeans, and flowery dresses. As I sauntered on, the sweet aroma of golden buns and thick almond-topped cookies on bakery racks filled my speed-burnt nostrils, along with the tangy smell in the fish markets of fresh mussels, clams, and oysters spread out on beds of ice.

I stopped and peered into the dimly lit stairwell going down to a mah-jongg parlor. Someday, I'd like to get up the nerve for that descent; the place screams "no trespassing."

Continuing my stroll through Chinatown, another touchy issue—this one resolved—pops into my head: I have "made it to the next level," as Havana says about all human interaction. When I first moved to San Francisco, I was put off after getting bumped and shoved by patrols of old Chinese women on Stockton yapping in Cantonese, toting home bulging plastic bags of chicken, pork, duck, plums, pears, oranges, melons, green beans, and giant heads of white cabbage. Doesn't bother me now, in fact I rather enjoy the granny assault, for I've come to believe this is not rudeness but their right, granted by age or custom or a mysterious power emanating across the Great Wall that I must respect.

I passed under the dragon-shaped arch at the entrance to Chinatown and headed into the Financial District. A bicycle messenger, girded up in tight black clothes and a silver helmet, zigzagged way too confidently around a Muni bus and a FedEx truck. Amid the deafening traffic, I jostled through the crowd in the late afternoon commute hour, picked up my pace, kept in step with earnest businessmen marching toward Landing Zone Delirious—the diagonal crosswalk at Montgomery and Sutter, the center of the beehive controlled by Mammon, a.k.a. Charles Schwab, his stock ticker hanging over the intersection, flashing its ever-changing Dow number.

Pillage on, day traders, you have nothing to lose but your Palm Pilots and Blackberries.

A woman at a table outside Caffe Bianco slipped off her high

heels, reached deep in a big tote bag, and pulled out her track tennies for the race down the BART escalator. The wind picked up as
I plunged ahead, rounded the corner on Market toward my destination: the flower stand.

In the explosion of red geraniums sending out their radiant glow,
I saw lilacs nodding toward my heart. I considered picking up an
armful of those lilacs. Instead, I sniffed the perfumes of desire
among all the flowers, held my breath, then plucked out a single
long-stemmed white rose.

Back at the Grant Building, I found Havana asleep on the futon
between white sheets, freshly laundered, smelling of sweet soap. An
apple on the table, her dress on the floor, the soaring crescendo of
Wagner's *Tannhäuser* filling the room. She's come to love that CD, a
gigantic next level up from drum and bass. I haven't said anything to
her about the dubious Nazi-Wagner link. She's still got the hots for
Hitler. I will continue to revisit this question with her as she continues to erase and redraw herself. The next level.

I sat down on the floor next to the futon, shook her shoulder. I
held the white rose under her nose. She stirred, blinked her eyes
open. I pressed the stem in her hand.

She smiled. Her eyes glistened. The orchestral surge softened.
Flutes faded away. She slid the flower across the sheet, placed it
between us. She took my hand in hers for a moment. Then her hand
slipped away, under her cheek, and she fell back asleep.

A moment? No, an eternity.

CLARIFICATION

Although *Vanilla Slim* is a work of nonfiction, I have in some cases drawn on my imagination and embellished the story. Here and there, time's arrow bends to my will; events that took place months or even years apart are scrambled together on these pages. The lunch at John's Grill is an example of recollection overtaken by a flight of fancy.

I ran this chapter past Lynn Myers. An e-mail from "Insight's" Deputy Editor followed.

I knew everything about me in Mr. Armstrong's book was suspect after he wrote "severe quotation marks" flew off my forefingers. I *never* do finger quotes. In fact, I abhor finger quotes.

And the waiter from Istanbul? Oh please, this is an obvious ploy so he can hype the already way-over-the-top purple prose with "the lustful Turk."

I drank one glass of wine, not three. Armstrong says when I ordered the wine, he immediately changed his mind and ordered a glass of Merlot. His action was more cowardly: He waited until he was halfway through lunch, and then finally had a beer.

I had a glass of Chardonnay, not Pinot Noir. His choice of red wine allowed him to introduce the ludicrous metaphor, "drops of virgin blood." I did not inhale a half-glass of wine in one gulp, nor did I spill any wine on my Jil Sander white shirt. I do not own a Jil Sander shirt.

ABOUT THE AUTHOR

Portrait of the pimp in jail.

ob Armstrong's stories have been published in the *San Francisco Chronicle* and numerous alternative newspapers. He writes a column for *Exotic,* a monthly adult magazine in Portland, Oregon. He divides his time between San Francisco and Portland.